mklifefit.

3 PHASES TO THE BEST SHAPE OF YOUR LIFE

An MK Personal Training Academy Book
Published by **Be Your Best** Publishing
PO Box 14787,
Shirley,
Solihull B90 9ES

www.mkpersonaltraining.co.uk
Tel/Fax: 0870 442 7115

ISBN: 978-0-9560407-0-1

BE YOUR BEST

forward_

If you are perusing this book right now it's odds on you are looking to make some changes to your life. You either want to lose weight, get a bit fitter or find a regime that cuts down on the excesses while still allowing for a reasonably enjoyable life style.

As we all know we need good air to breath, clean water to drink and healthy food to eat. But there is a fourth aspect that is often overlooked and that is MOVEMENT. It may surprise you but the body needs movement just as much as the other three. Try being confined to your bed for a month and see the problems your body will develop, wasting of the muscles, a downturn in flexibility, joint pain, headaches and an overall sluggishness that saps the soul. OK, so you don't spend that much time in bed, but the lack of regular exercise can bring on some, if not all, of these problems to some degree.

This is where Matt Kendrick and his team come to the fore. In this book Matt deals with all four aspects with a combination of experience, knowledge and understanding. He knows you will cheat a little it's only human nature but providing you can keep it in check, spend a little willpower resisting the junk and excesses of life, he has a system that will work for you. It is not THAT arduous but it will need a certain amount of responsible effort to achieve results. Let's face it there is no magic pill or 10 minutes a week routine that is going to change things for you, if you think otherwise I've got some Enron shares you can buy; it's time to get real and make the effort. He will take you through a procedure that is right for you, the correct exercise to achieve your goals, whether you want a trim figure or Arnold Schwarzenegger type muscles. The correct foods to eat to maintain the gains you have worked for and a constant monitoring to keep you up to scratch.

I have been with Matt for three and half years now and can highly recommend his methods. I have over the last 30 years accumulated a fair knowledge of food, vitamins and minerals and health matters much of which coincides with Matt's understanding and learning, so I know he knows what he is talking about. By adopting a steady training routine, one hour three times a week under his tuition, I now have a training age 25 years younger than my own. I feel great, I have a vitality that many of my friends of the same age envy and I know I am doing the right thing. Sure it takes a bit of effort, but it's worth it.

There is much in this book that is life prolonging. Follow its common sense and you will have a good chance of avoiding the ills that are associated with a Western way of living and sedentary lifestyle. Good Health!

Jasper Carrott.
OBE.MA

contents_

The Big Question:

ARE YOU TRULY READY TO CHANGE YOUR LIFESTYLE?

introduction_

Stop, think; what does that mean?

To improve your health, how you feel, how you look, to be happy with how your body looks uncovered.

Do you believe that's possible?

By following the phases within this book you can achieve all this and much more. Ultimately preventing disease and living healthily.

But are you ready?
Think about your reasons...

To be free of any pain, or inflammation, fit enough to enjoy and be involved in any activity you wish or perhaps watching your children and grandchildren growing up. Free to feel true energy and vitality every day. Free to enjoy the fruits of your labour when you retire. Or simply 'to no longer dread showing your body in your swimsuit or trunks'. To buy clothes you love, rather than those that hide what's underneath.

Now whenever you feel weakness through the phases ahead, remember '***your***' reasons.

When you are ready, clear out the cupboards of any cheat foods and drinks that are not on the plan.
Remove temptation.

Note to parents

Try having a separate cupboard for the kids, but remember, keep their naughty foods to a minimum, only buy enough for their week's intake, leaving no extras for yourselves.

"We are indeed much more than what we eat, but what we eat can nevertheless help us to be much more than what we are"
Adelle Davis

LOOK OUT FOR OUR HEALTHY KIDS MENUS

so, why lifefit?

the right Protein
Lean and healthy.

the right Carbohydrates
Low glycemic and fibrous.

the right Fats
Unsaturated and anti-inflammatory.

the right Meals
Combined to feed lean fat burning muscle tissue and burn stubborn body fat.

the right Times
To keep blood sugar levels stable and raise metabolic rate.

Disclaimer
Before beginning this diet and exercise program, consult with your G.P. to ensure you are in proper health. This book is not meant to provide medical advice. No liability is assumed for any information contained here in.

top tip
Always train with weights/resistance first in the workout and cardio/CV afterwards for maximum fat burning effect.

setting your goals_

Firstly, have a clear idea of what shape you would like to be in and imagine exactly how you will look and just how confident you will feel. The notes pages at the back of the book help keep a log of the journey.

Remember, your goals are personal and may be about body image, health, sport or just simply feeling better.

The long-term goal may seem so far off. That is why small short-term goals help you to constantly achieve results.

At **MK Personal Training Academy** we assess results every 4 weeks to help our clients stay motivated and on track.

- Set specific goals.
- Set measurable goals.
- Set big goals.
- Set realistic deadlines.
- Set long-term and short-term goals.
- Establish emotional reasons why you want to achieve your goals.
- Focus on one goal at a time.

real goal examples_

for women

I fit perfectly into that little black dress.

I eat 5 meals a day with the proper healthy ratios always at regular intervals.

I stay well hydrated and purify my body by drinking my water allowance each day.

I can't wait to wear my bikini when I hit the beach.

for men

I can see all of my toes when I look down!

I am reaching my ideal weight and body composition by April, so I can show off my beach body.

I am keeping up these lifestyle changes when the 12 weeks are over to be as healthy as I can be.

your goals_

weekly:

4 weekly:

your goals_

12 weekly:

long term:

the 3 phases_

Phase 1

This is for 2 short weeks and will cleanse the body of toxins as you kick start the fat loss process. Green Foods Only.

Phase 2

This is for 4 weeks as the transitional phase is here, your healthy habits replace poor old ones. Your metabolism is now shifting nicely, allowing some cheat time back in.

Phase 3

This 6 week phase – From Here to Eternity – is designed to help with additional cheat time, not sabotage all of that good life changing work.

Why 12 weeks?

Most body transformation programs seem to be based on 6 weeks, so why is ours 12? Simply because it is not just about transforming the body, but truly changing mindset and lifestyle.

Follow MK Lifefit through to Week 12 and we promise you that the way you look and feel will have changed forever!

how to make the 3 Phase Plan work for you_

The importance of eating consistently

The secret of losing the body fat permanently is keeping a regular eating pattern, Monday to Sunday.

Weekdays are easier to develop routine, eating 3 meals and 2 snacks, but it is the weekends where we tend to slip up.

We find many clients follow the plan during the week religiously, only to have an 'entire' cheat weekend at the end of it!

Here's how to do it:

- Think of where you will be tomorrow and plan the day in advance.
- Schedule a time for each meal or snack and stick to it.
- Cook in bulk.
- Plan ahead when travelling.

2 choices:

1_

Pick a meal, e.g; breakfast or dinner, where you have most time.

For example, if this is dinner time, cook your evening meal and the meals for the next day, or you can cook extra from the evening meal for lunch etc.

2_

Cook your protein in batches, chicken, turkey breast etc. refrigerate over the week with salads.

For example, Wednesdays and Sundays, allow 90 mins to make large salads to last 3 days and cook up enough protein to refrigerate.

"ACT AS IF IT WERE IMPOSSIBLE TO FAIL"

Dorothea Brande

the PSP_

top tip:
If you buy it you will eat it so don't buy hungry, buy healthy!

Planning

– Sunday – Cook Day
Wednesday – Cook Day

Shopping

– Saturday/Sunday

Prepping

– Slice up veggies – store in containers
Cook chicken/turkey etc – portion and season

kitchen tools_

Kitchen tools to make life easier:

Steamer: A real healthy way to cook. Helps save all the nutrients and better still, you can set the timer and get on with other things.

George Foreman Grill: Cooking temperature a little high, but a great time saver.

Tupperware: Small and large air tight food containers and shakers – essential for your shakes at snack time and great to store veggies etc.

Blender: JML – blender and juicer in one – the smoothies taste so good blended.

Ziploc bags: Great for keeping nuts and seeds for snacking during the day.

Digital scales: oz and grams – follow our recipes exactly and soon you will know without weighing.

Measuring cups and spoons:
As above.

Juicer: A great way to drink all your vitamins and antioxidants.

Wok: Stir-frys are healthy, quick and easy.

the 7 habits of healthy lean people_

1. Always eat every 3 hours. A minimum 5 meals per day.
2. Eat protein at every meal or snack.
3. Carbohydrates mainly come from vegetables and fruit.
4. At least 20% of energy is from fat – mainly monounsaturated (olive oil) and polyunsaturated (fish, flax oil, nuts and seeds).
5. Drinks come from non calorie beverages – Water.
6. We are designed to move – exercise is not an option.
7. Enjoy cheating 10% of the time until you have reached your goals.

the **5** reasons to eat regularly_

1. **Eating every 3-4 hours** speeds up you metabolism due to the thermic effect of food.
2. **Eating every 3-4** hours controls food craving and prevents binge eating.
3. **Eating every 3-4** hours keeps blood sugar levels stable and provides consistently high energy levels.
4. **Eating every 3-4 hours** promotes fat burning muscle tone growth and prevents muscle breakdown.
5. **Eating every 3-4 hours** reduces fat storage through portion size control.

"MOTIVATION IS WHAT GETS YOU STARTED. HABIT IS WHAT KEEPS YOU GOING"

Jim Ryan

the big 3_
the macro-nutrients:

Protein (amino acids) – Lean
Carbohydrates – Low Glycemic
Fats – Essential Fatty Acids

Protein – Meaning "of first importance" is essential for muscle tissue, growth and repair, the formation of bone, skin and hair. Generally we tend to eat the wrong kind of protein; high fat red meats, cows dairy, processed sandwich meats. Lean, un-denatured protein, such as chicken, turkey, fish, eggs, cottage cheese and whey is best, containing the 8 essential and 12 non essential amino acids.

Carbohydrates – The fuel, without doubt the main culprit behind the rapid rise in obesity, is high sugar, quick fix 'simple carbs'. As we become more aware of the dangers of sugar, food manufacturers get more clever at hiding it, preferring us to concentrate on low fat. Low glycemic carbohydrates provide us with all the energy we need, nice and slowly preventing blood sugar swings.

Fats – We obsess about avoiding these due to the calorie amounts, but we need to understand the difference between saturated and unsaturated. Saturated fats are solid at room temperature, such as butter, lard and should be used sparingly. 2 types of unsaturated are monounsaturated and polyunsaturated. Monounsaturated, such as olive oil, avocado, are healthy as proven in Mediterranean Countries. Polyunsaturated fats, known as EFAs are present in flax and fish oils and nuts and seeds. Research has shown these can help prevent heart disease, diabetes, MS etc.

We need a balance of fats (even saturated) with much focus on the EFAs that our bodies need and can't produce ourselves.

top tip

A protein shake within the first 15 minutes of finishing your workout stops muscle breakdown and fuels fat loss.

good protein_

Fish

- Anchovies
- Bream
- Brill
- Carp
- Cod
- Dover sole
- Grey mullet
- Haddock
- Hake
- Halibut
- Herring
- Hoki
- Lemon sole
- Mackerel
- Mahi mahi
- Marlin
- Monkfish
- Perch
- Plaice
- Red mullet
- Salmon
- Sardine
- Sea bass
- Sea bream
- Skate
- Swordfish
- Trout
- Tuna
- Turbot
- Whitebait

Meat

- Chicken
- Turkey
- Lean beef (sparingly)

Vegetarian

- Pulses-lentils black beans, Adzuki beans etc.
- Quorn
- Tofu

Dairy

- Cottage cheese
- Live natural yoghurt
- Feta cheese
- Mozzarella cheese (made from buffalo milk)
- Goat's milk
- Goat's milk yoghurt

Free range organic eggs

Non-dairy foods

- Almond milk
- Oat milk
- Rice milk
- Soya milk
- Soya yoghurt

Protein to avoid/limit

- Duck
- Ham
- Cheese
- Bacon
- Pork
- Milk
- Ground beef
- Luncheon meat

good carbs_

Fruit

Apples
Apricots
Banana
Blackberries
Blackcurrants
Cranberries
Strawberries
Blueberries
Cherries Red and White
Grapes
Mandarins
Mangoes
Oranges
Papayas
Peaches
Pineapple
Satsumas
Tangerines

Grains

Quinoa

Vegetables

Asparagus
Artichokes
Beans, broad, green runner
Broccoli
Brussel sprouts
Cabbage red and green
Cauliflower
Greens
Kale
Leeks
Pak choi
Spinach

Salads

Bean sprouts
Celery
Chicory
Lettuce
Mushrooms
Peppers, red, orange or yellow
Rocket
Spinach
Sprouted seeds and beans eg alfalfa, mung
Avocados
Beetroot

good fats_

Nuts and seeds	Cold pressed oils
Almonds	Extra virgin olive oil
Brazils	Flaxseed (linseed)
Cashews	Udo's flax oil
Hazelnuts	Borage, hemp
Linseeds (flaxseeds)	Pumpkin seed
Macadamias	Rapeseed
Pecans	Sesame
Pine nuts	Sunflower
Pumpkin seeds	Walnut
Seasame seeds	
Sunflower seeds	
Walnuts	

Fats to avoid/limit

- Processed vegetable oils
- Hydrogenated or partially hydrogenated
- Fried foods
- Margarines

your shopping list_

Protein:

Cottage cheese
Feta
Free range chicken
Free range turkey
Fresh fish – especially;
Salmon, Cod, Sole, Haddock
Tuna and Mackeral
Free range eggs
Lean red meats
Liquid egg whites
Mozzarella
Whey

Carbs:

Grains
Brown rice
Gluten-free flour
Millet flakes
Oats, plain
Quinoa
Rye/wholegrain bread

Fruit
Apples
Apricots
Banana
Blackberries
Blackcurrants
Cranberries
Strawberries
Blueberries
Cherries
Red and White
Grapes
Mandarins
Mangoes
Oranges
Papayas
Peaches
Pineapple
Satsumas
Tangerines
Frozen fruit

Vegetables
Asparagus
Avocados
Beansprouts
Beetroot, baby
Broccoli
Cabbage, green, red and white
Carrots
Celeriac
Celery
Chinese leaves
Corn, baby cobs
Courgettes
Cucumbers
Fennel, florence
Garlic
Green beans
Lettuce, romaine or cos
Mangetout
Mixed salad leaves
Mushrooms, white and brown
Onions, yellow and red
Peas, frozen
Peppers, red, yellow and green
Red chillies, fresh
Rocket
Shallot
Spinach
Spring Onions
Sprouted seeds
Squash, butternut
Sugar snap peas
Sweet potato

Pulses
Butter beans, canned
Cannellini beans canned
Chick peas canned
Flageolet beans, canned
Lentils
Black beans
Mixed beans, canned
Mung beans, dried
Red kidney beans
Split yellow lentils, dried
Split yellow peas, dried
Hummus

Fats:

Nuts and seeds
Almonds
Brazil nuts
Cashew nuts
Hazelnuts
Linseeds
Pine nuts
Pumpkin, seasame and
Sunflower seeds
Walnuts
Pecans
Macadamias

Oils
Avocado oil
Extra virgin olive oil
Seasame oil
Walnut oil
Flax oil

Key:
Green =
Phase 1 items

your shopping list_

Herbs and spices:

Herbs
Basil
Bay leaves
Chives
Corriander
Dill
Fennel
Lemon grass
Marjoram
Mint
Mixed herbs, dried
Oregano, dried
Parsley
Rosemary
Sage
Thyme
Black pepper
Caraway seeds
Cayenne
Chilli paste
Chilli powder
Cinnamon, ground
Cinnamon, sticks
Cloves
Coriander seeds
Cumin seeds
Fennel seeds
Five-spice paste
Ginger (fresh)
Mustard seed (black)

Key:
Green = Phase 1 items

Store cupboard essentials:

Black olives
Coconut, milk
Honey, manuka – unpasteurised
Horseradish sauce
Mixed vegetable juice
Mustard, dijon
Mustard, wholegrain
Peanut butter – natural
Soy sauce
Stock, fish
Stock, vegetable
Stock powder
Sun-dried tomatoes in olive oil
Tomato paste
Tomatoes, canned
Vinegar, balsamic
Vinegar, cider
Vinegar, red wine

Beverages:

Mineral water
Green tea
Rooibos tea
Ame/Elderflower
Herbal teas
Dandelion coffee
Pure fruit juice
Pure vegetable juice

lifestyle structure_

The daily essentials

Sleep_

Fact: Lack of sleep interferes with fat loss and ultimately health. Important times: 10.30pm-6.30am, get as close to these times as possible.

Nutrition_

Quality and quantity of food, frequency of meals.

Exercise_

Fact: Muscle burns calories (use it or lose it).

Natural Health Products_

Vitamins, minerals, enzymes, essential fatty acids, whey.

Water_

Fact: Hydration is critical to every function of the body, dehydration interferes with fat loss.

The daily battles

When day to day life interferes to throw you off_

Restless sleep, work stress, business trips, social commitments (fun time!)

Learning to build this in with:

Relationships (family etc)	–	Time commitments
Work	–	Time commitments

Remember your goals, how far you have come, why you started.

optimal blood sugar_

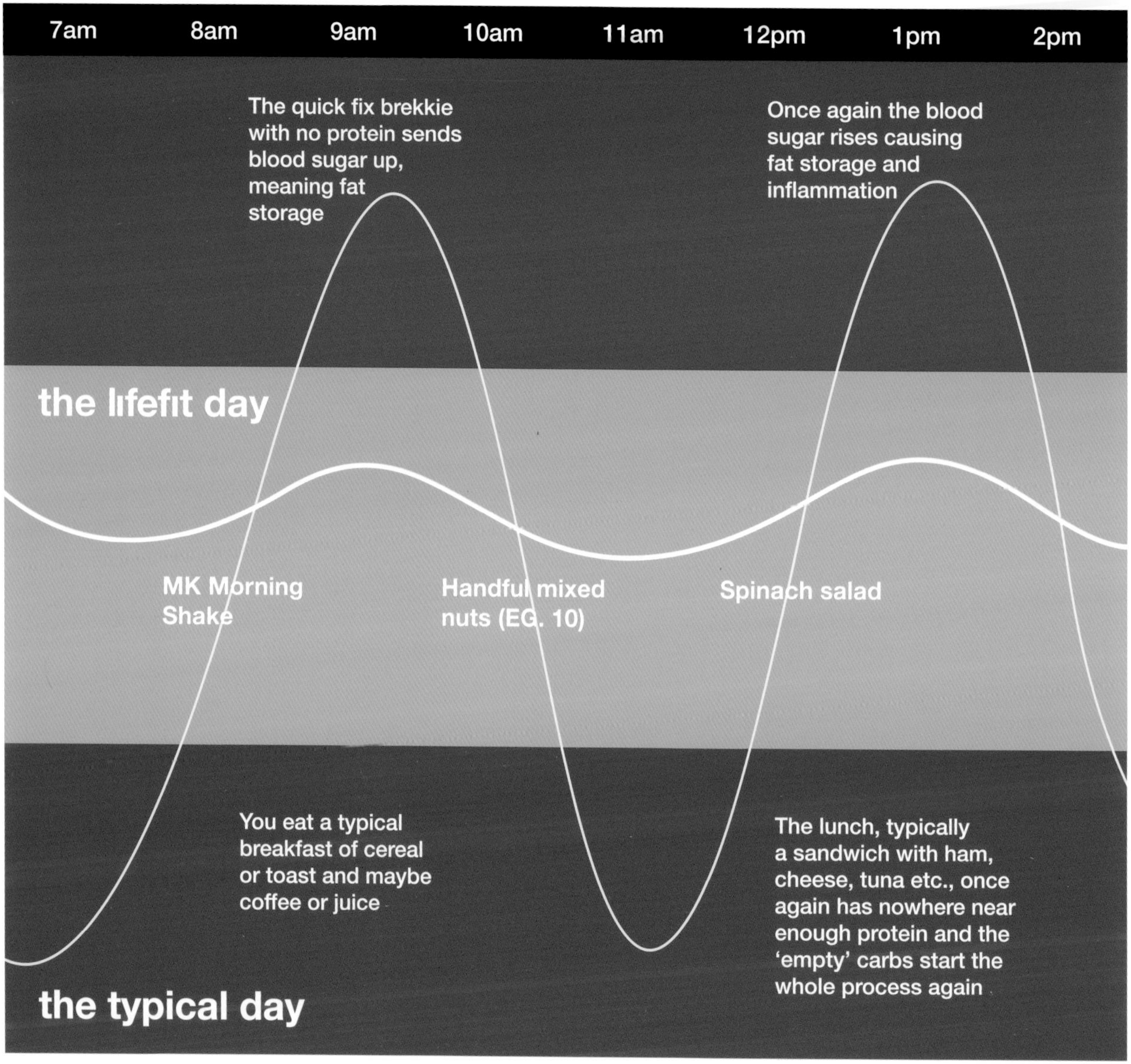

GREEN = Stable blood sugar, positive nitrogen balance (muscle sparing), fat burning

RED = Fluctuating blood sugar, negative nitrogen balance (muscle burning), fat storing

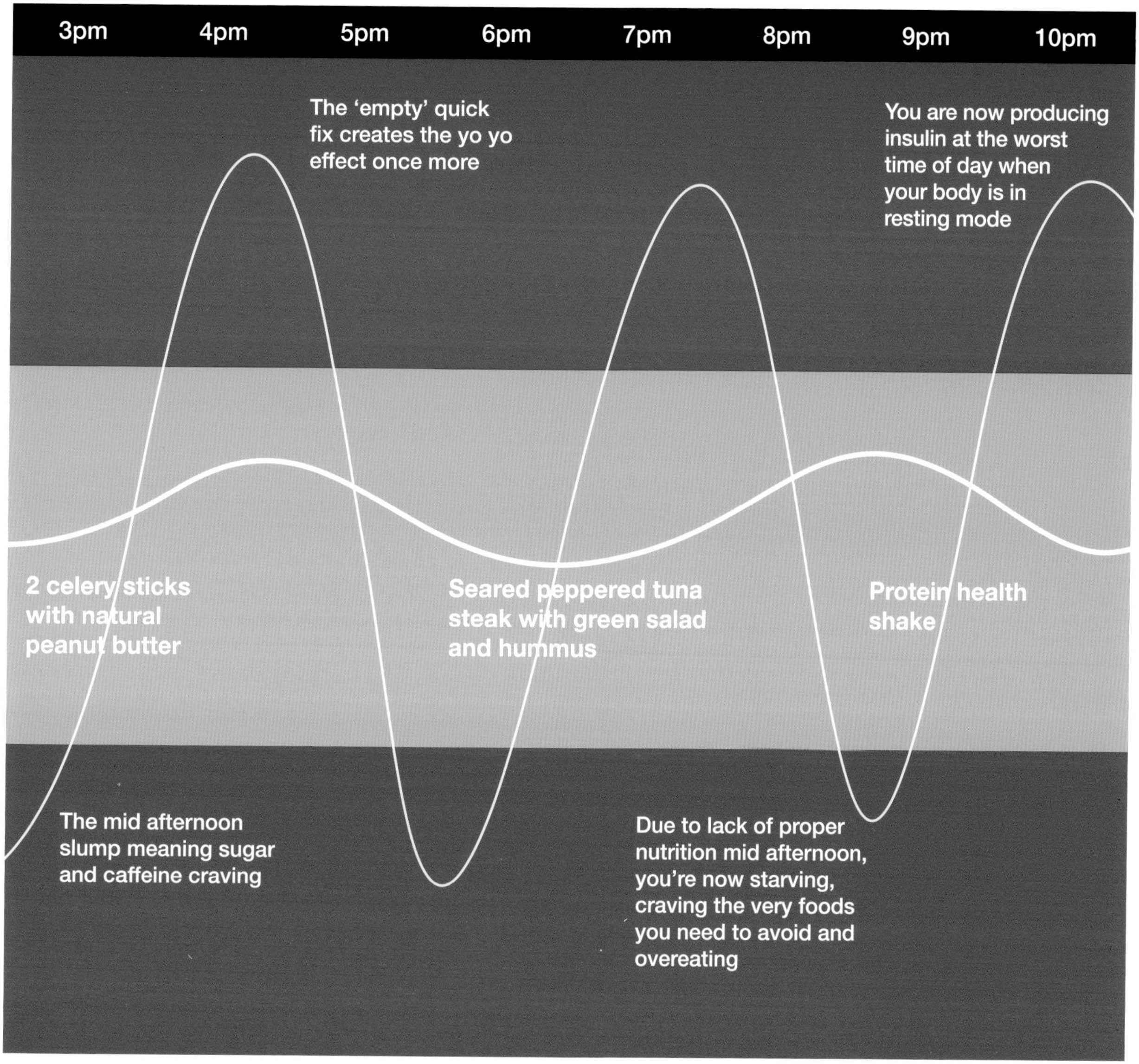
3pm
4pm
5pm
6pm
7pm
8pm
9pm
10pm
The 'empty' quick fix creates the yo yo effect once more
You are now producing insulin at the worst time of day when your body is in resting mode
2 celery sticks with natural peanut butter
Seared peppered tuna steak with green salad and hummus
Protein health shake
The mid afternoon slump meaning sugar and caffeine craving
Due to lack of proper nutrition mid afternoon, you're now starving, craving the very foods you need to avoid and overeating

Eddie's story_

Below are the medical results for a client of **MK Personal Training Academy**. Eddie came to see me after the initial results and was determined to make changes before it was too late.

In a short space of time, with a large dose of determination and by following the nutrition and training advice contained in this book, Eddie made fantastic progress.

"The regular eating was far easier than I imagined, giving me loads of energy and the training programs were designed to fit into my busy schedule. I can honestly say that I have never felt better, and to discover I was not diabetic was fantastic."

Eddie Rai

August 2007	*Medical results*
Oral GTT Before glucose drink: 7.3 2 hours after glucose drink: 12.8	**What this means:** Diabetic
Weight Weight: 92.5kg BMI: 30.9	**What this means:** You are obese
Waist circumference Result: 99cm	**What this means:** You are overweight and at risk from diabetes
Blood pressure Systolic/Diastolic BP 135/83	**What this means:** Normal blood pressure
Cholesterol Total cholesterol – 5.4	**What this means:** Total cholesterol is too high and you are at risk from a heart attack

October 2007	*Medical results*
Oral GTT Before glucose drink: 5.4 2 hours after glucose drink: 7.8	**What this means:** Blood sugar is higher than normal, but not high enough to detect diabetes.
Weight Weight: 86kg BMI: 28.7	**What this means:** Your BMI is showing that you are overweight.
Waist circumference Result: 93cm	**What this means:** Waist measurement is normal.
Blood pressure Systolic/Diastolic BP 129/81	**What this means:** Normal blood pressure
Cholesterol Total cholesterol – 3.6	**What this means:** Total cholesterol is normal

Val's story_

Val joined **MK Personal Training Academy** with the goal of shaping up for her forthcoming wedding. After assessing Val's individual needs, we worked on improving the all important posture and muscle tone for her to dazzle on the big day.

As you can see the results speak for themselves:

Date:	17/03/08	09/05/08
Weight:	11st 6 lbs	10st 11 lbs
Waist:	37 ins	32 ins
Hip:	40.75 ins	38.5 ins
Thigh:	23 ins	22.5 ins
Arm:	13.25 ins	11.25 ins
Calf:	15.5 ins	15 ins

"After years of trying different diets, which resulted in a quick fix, I am really pleased that I decided to do things properly. Without MK Personal Training Academy I would never have been able to achieve my goal which was to lose weight and tone up for my forthcoming wedding."

Val Platt

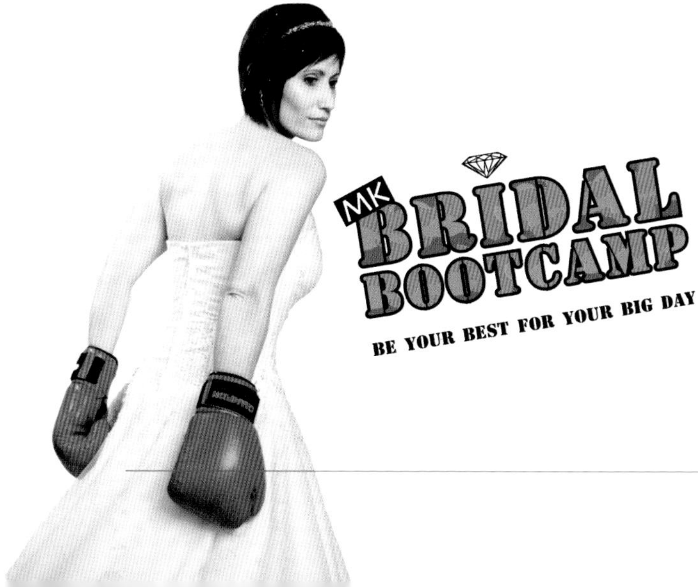

This is a unique opportunity to be your absolute best on your most special day. Let us help you to get into the best shape of your life while you're having fun and enjoying constant pampering. At the end of the course we'll reward you with a make over and a pre-wedding photo shoot.

For more information please call us on: 0870 442 7115

Mark's story_

46 year old Mark joined **MK Personal Training Academy** ready to truly change his lifestyle. Mark had spent the previous 20 years striving for business success with little time to focus on himself. He wholeheartedly took on the nutrition alongside the training.

Below are Mark's results and he has not looked back since.

Date:	14/03/04	14/05/04
Weight:	88 kg	82.7 kg
Bodyfat:	24.2%	18%
Waist:	35 ins	32 ins

"After 12 weeks I felt 10 years younger! The food plan gave me energy and vitality I never knew existed and the training although tough was inspiring. I now can't imagine a different lifestyle."

Mark Winter

Simon's story_

Simon joined **MK Personal Training Academy** as a regular exerciser who found the harder he worked the more frustrated with lack of results he became. Sounds like the majority of gym users.

We set about building the nutrition principles alongside structured resistance training and wow! …what a difference.

Date:	07/01/08	30/04/08
Weight:	13 st 6 lbs	11 st 12 lbs
Bodyfat:	25.3%	19%
Waist:	39.5 ins	35 ins

"Three months ago, I was typical of most people in a sedentary job, overweight and out of condition. Since then, by simply following the advice of MK, I have transformed my body, posture, energy levels and emotional well being. I still have goals to achieve, but now know exactly what I need to do to get there. For me, the MK programme has given me a lot more than the 'normal' exercise and diet regime, it's taught me how to live my life in a healthier way."

Simon Mills

Jackie's story_

Jackie came to see us just after giving birth to her second child and feeling the need to shed the excess baby weight. We set about strengthening the deep tummy muscles and posture muscles to help with busy motherhood, while the combination of regular eating of the right foods and effective fat loss training did the rest.

Date:	01/10/02	01/12/02
Weight:	154 lbs	140 lbs
Bodyfat:	25.5%	21%
Waist:	33 ins	29 ins

"After my second pregnancy, though overjoyed, I felt exhausted and fat! I was recommended MK Personal Training Academy through a friend and when Matt told me what was possible I didn't believe him! Exercise and proper nutrition are now just part of my life but that still enables me 'cheat time' for pure indulgence. I am now in the very best shape of my life, in my thirties with three children."

Jackie Smith

Cheryl's story_

When Cheryl came into **MK Personal Training Academy** to see us, she was using the gym regularly, not in need of real weight loss just toning. Like most females Cheryl was mainly doing classes and feared weights would make her bulky. The results below show what we already knew as Cheryl dropped any excess fat and improved muscle tone.

Date:	01/03/08	18/05/08
Weight:	10 st 8 lbs	10 st 3 lbs
Waist:	33.5 ins	30.5 ins
Hips:	40.5 ins	39 ins
Thigh:	21.5 ins	21 ins
Arm:	13 ins	11.25 ins
Calf:	14 ins	14 ins

"Having always been in to going to the gym regularly, I was really frustrated that I couldn't shed that 'extra stubborn bit'. By following the regular eating plans and changing from classes to resistance training, with MK Personal Training Academy I was amazed just how easily it came off."

Cheryl Taylor

a word on water_

Two thirds of what we weigh is water. We can live for weeks without food, but only a few days without water, as it keeps all functions of the body working.

Always try to drink water at regular intervals through the day and have a bottle with you, as a rule, try a glass every hour or so.

Most of us are chronically dehydrated and do not realise, it can be the cause of symptoms, such as weight gain, cellulite, high blood pressure, headaches, tiredness etc.

Just five glasses of water daily can decrease our risk of colon cancer, breast cancer and bladder cancer. Natural mineral water is full of nutrients and reverse osmosis is the most cost effective, cleanest water available.

For more information, refer to back of book.

a word on alcohol_

Alcohol is 7 kcals per gram, second only to fat in terms of calorie density, so it needs to be included in your calorie quota.

You can follow the food and exercise plan perfectly and due to alcohol content, not lose a single pound!

Remember – moderation is defined as 1-2 drinks per sitting.

Alcohol is a diuretic, meaning it dehydrates you. This will stop you burning fat, so drink an extra glass of water for every alcoholic drink.

Drink no more than once or twice a week.

If you are on one of those special occasions, when drinking more, then follow each drink with a glass of water and try to have a protein shake before bed.

2 DRINKS EVERY DAY IS 14 DRINKS PER WEEK = TOO MANY

eat low fat_
get fat

Something is amiss… we have more low fat food than ever and more obesity than ever!

Over the last 15-20 years, low fat food has become more and more popular due to promotion through the media that fat as a nutrient causes obesity and heart disease.

The fact that fat is 9 kcals per gram, with carbohydrates only 4 kcals per gram, worked perfectly into the myth as people concentrated on weight loss not fat loss. It is no surprise to find diabetes is on the rise, almost at the same rate as obesity, as low fat food is generally high in sugar.

A good rule to remember is "could our ancestors eat it?" or "was it available thousands of years ago?", if not, it is probably not that good for us.

top tip
Workouts should consist of exercises involving many muscle groups not isolation movements.

know what you are eating_

"IGNORANCE IS BLISS, BUT KNOWLEDGE IS POWER."

Such a true statement, I know where I want to be. If we understand food and we know exactly what we are eating most of the time, I genuinely believe we cannot go wrong.

Remember - this is all about health and empowering each and everyone of us.

A SIMPLE BUT VERY EFFECTIVE RULE – 1 BASIC NATURAL INGREDIENT.

If you don't know what is going in your food, you don't really know what you are eating.

Tuna = Tuna
Almond Nut = Almond Nut

Below are examples of supposed healthy food that contain far more than the 1 basic natural ingredients.

See opposite page for our example.

Remember you can lose weight eating a weight watchers cake or dessert but you are not losing fat or gaining health.

Low fat pasta tomato sauce = tomatoes, tomato puree, onion, celery, modified maize starch, lemon juice from concentrate, sugar, salt, kibbled onion, garlic puree, sunflower oil, basil, acidity regulator, oregano, flavouring (normally too many chemicals to list.)

Muller Healthy Balance low fat yoghurt = Yoghurt, water, sugar, peach puree, corn starch, natural flavourings. Carbohydrate – 13.6g (of which is sugar – 12.8g)

Special K = Rice, wheat, sugar, wheat gluten, defatted wheatgerm, dried skimmed milk, salt, barley malt flavouring, vit c, niacin, iron, vit b6, b2, b1, folic acid, b1. Carbohydrate per 100gm – 75g (17g of which is sugar, 58 g of which is starch)

Our example_

Tuna kebab with stir fry vegetables and hummus

1 x 200g fresh tuna
1 x red pepper
1 x bag bean sprouts
1 x onion sliced
1 x carrot sliced
1 x bag mange tout
1 x 100g hummus
2 x kebab sticks
1 x bunch basil
1 x clove garlic
1 x bunch coriander
1 x 2 tbsp olive oil

REAL FOOD

the calorie thing_

Protein	- 1 gm =	**4 kcals**
Carbs	- 1 gm =	**4 kcals**
Fat	- 1 gm =	**9 kcals**
Alcohol	- 1 gm =	**7 kcals**

We are calorie obsessed. Counting calories does not work on its own, we need to take into account the difference between food types. However, if we eat more calories than we burn off, we don't achieve results. Be careful when picking at food not on the phase/plan.

Don't be tricked by the diet industry.

Diets don't work. It's not about losing weight, it's about losing FAT. A calorie is not just a calorie. When we work on calories alone, we ignore the different effects of proteins, carbs and fats on our bodies.

By reducing our calories right down, our metabolism slows to cope and we end up storing more fat. As we return to typical eating habits, we regain the weight and more.

We would rather create a smaller deficit, 500 kcals daily max = 1-2lbs of fat per week. A combination of whole food nutrition and resistance training to provide steady permanent fat loss.

Lean protein is **FAT BURNING** – 4 kcals per gram

High glycemic carbohydrates are **FAT STORING** – 4 kcals per gram

Please refer to our website for daily tracking:

www.mkpersonaltraining.co.uk

the "I've got no time" section_

"Hail the power of the protein smoothie"

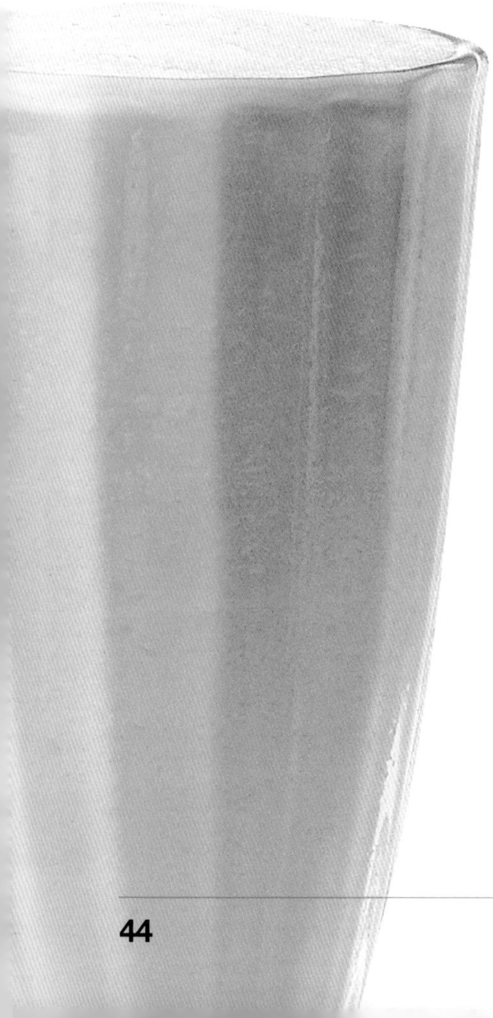

Protein is absolutely crucial to our health and directly affects how we look and feel.

Unlike fat and carbohydrate it is not stored and must be partitioned in the right quantity throughout the day to prevent fat storage, muscle loss and fatigue.

This idea of shakes is very alien to us, but then we think nothing of putting all sorts of rubbish into our mouths!

Homemade shakes are a fantastic time saver, teaming with vitamins, minerals and antioxidants to keep us healthy and lean.

- 1-2 scoops whey protein isolate
- 1-2 dessert spoons cold pressed flax oil
- Handful fresh blueberries
- 250 ml water

“AVOIDING THE PHRASE **‘I DON’T HAVE TIME’** WILL SOON HELP YOU REALISE THAT YOU DO HAVE THE TIME NEEDED FOR JUST ABOUT ANYTHING YOU CHOOSE TO ACCOMPLISH IN LIFE.”

Bo Bennet

drink your 3 factors of health_

Juices and smoothies are a great way to pack in vitamins and minerals to your diet. Remember, from a body fat perspective, you will need to **add some protein**. (e.g. whey).

For the juice you will need a press or juicer and for the smoothie a blender.

Energy blast:

Fruit juice_
Awesome Apple

1 apple
1 nectarine
8 strawberries

Smoothie_
Banana bliss

2 banana
1 tsp cocoa powder
1/2 tsp vanilla extract
1 tsp honey
1/2 cup live yoghurt
1/2 cup pineapple juice

Immune booster:

Fruit juice_
Grapefruit goodness

1-2 grapefruits
1 lemon
1 lime

Smoothie_
Mango magic

1 mango
1 grapefruit
1/2 inch grated ginger root
1/2 cup apple juice

Digestive healer:

Fruit juice_
Ginger goodness

1-2 pears
1-2 carrots
1/2 pineapple
1/2 inch ginger root

Smoothie_
Sweet soother

5 apricots
1/2 lime juice
1/2 cup prune juice

supplements_

Keep in mind that unfortunately even "a very good diet" does not provide us with everything needed. Modern life environment, now has more pollutants and toxins than ever before and we need to arm ourselves with natural health products to fight free radicals and boost our body's defences.

How often are we told by the medical world or media that we get everything we need from food? Given the choice what would you rather be, at the bare minimum of health just getting by, or thriving with energy and vitality at optimum level?

For the past 30 years, countless respected validated studies have shown that, by using multi nutrient supplements, we can boost immunity, improve childhood development, reduce colds, balance moods, stop PMS, increase energy and vitality and most importantly, reduce the risk of cancer, heart disease thus providing a long and healthy life.

At **MK Personal Training Academy**, we believe that supplements are very important for anyone exercising due to the added stress this places on the body (note – the benefits far outweigh this). We also passionately believe in stringent safety standards and quality control, which is why we decided to design our own.

Unfortunately, the quality standards are too often lacking and we pride ourselves on using one of only a handful of ISO 9001 quality assured manufacturers in the UK.

For more info please contact: MK Personal Training Academy 0870 442 7115

mklifefit.
anti inflammatory
Fish oils containing EPA and DHA are now recognised as helpful in the maintenance of joint flexibility, heart health and supporting brain function throughout our life time.
Fish Oil Capsules
120 Capsules
mklifefit.

the basics_

Whey protein isolate – The most un-dernatured, clean and highest biological value of all protein, meaning your body can retain and utilise the positive nitrogen better than in eggs, meat, fish and soy. Whey protein isolate boosts immune function better than any other protein.

Essential fatty acids – These omega 3 fats are critical to health which the body cannot make on its own. Helps prevent cardiovascular disease, and block disease related inflammatory responses in the body, helping also to lower blood pressure.

The 2 main types are:

Fish oil

The two most potent forms of omega 3 – (EPA) and (DHA) are found in abundance In cold water fish such as salmon, trout, mackerel and sardines.

Flax oil

The essential fatty acid found in flax seeds - alpha linolenic acid.

Multi vitamins and minerals – These are organic substances necessary for life and when consumed in or along with foods they are taken into our bodies and become necessary for activating thousands of bodily functions. You are short-changing yourself if you believe that your diet can or will supply you with everything you need, even if you eat an organic diet.

Glucosamine – Found in high amounts in the joints and connective tissues, for cartilage maintenance and repair. Relieves pain, stiffness and swelling of the back, hips, knees, fingers and other joints, caused by osteoarthritis and rheumatoid arthritis. Very effective as a prevention tool.

Probiotics – The gut contains billions of bacteria. They play a vital role in normal digestive function, lowering blood cholesterol levels and improving healthy immune response. Probiotics come in the form of a capsule that acts as 'friendly bacteria' able to compete against the harmful micro-organisms, resulting in a healthier gut function.

calculating your basal metabolic rate_

Your Basal Metabolic Rate (BMR) is the number of calories that your body burns in a 24 hour period, while doing nothing. That means if you were sleeping or watching TV for 24 hours, this is the amount of calories you would burn.

This figure, combined with the activity factor, will give you a very good idea of how many calories per day you need to maintain weight. Adjust accordingly.

Men = 66 + (13.7 x weight in kg) + (5 x height in cm) – (6.8 x age)

Women = 655 + (9.6 x weight in kg) + (1.8 x height in cm) – (4.7 x age)

Notes
1 inch = 2.54 cm
1 kg = 2.2 lbs

Activity Factor

BMR x 1.2 = If you are sedentary (no exercise all day)
BMR x 1.375 = Light activity (exercise 1-3 days per week)
BMR x 1.55 = Moderately active (exercise 3-5 days per week)
BMR x 1.725 = Very active (exercise/sports 6-7 days per week)
BMR x 1.9 = Very high activity (twice a day training, sports and training or training and demanding job)

MK Personal Training Academy can provide exact figures based on accurate measurements of your lean body mass.

your individual guidelines_

Please contact: MK Personal Training Academy to discover your exact needs.

On the MK Lifefit program we recommend a general daily ratio of 50% Carbohydrates, 30% Protein and 20% Fat. You can calculate this now you have your daily calories and fill in below. Track using **www.mkpersonaltraining.co.uk**.

blood type: ______________ body type: ______________

metabolic type: ______________

special considerations: ______________

____

supplement recommendations: ______________

____

macro-nutrient ratios %: ***(carbs: 40-50%, protein: 30-40%, fat: 20-30%)***

____

daily Kcals: ______________

meal timings: ***breakfast*** ______________ ***snack*** ______________

snack ______________ ***dinner*** ______________

lunch ______________ ***snack*** ______________

ORGANIC IS BEST

Non organic produce is routinely grown using chemical fertilisers and pesticides linked to all manner of health problems. Non organic meat and fish is often reared with growth hormones and the animals are fed cheap grains to make them fatter and more profitable. These animals have not evolved to eat poor quality food and this will often lead to the animal storing toxins and a greater risk of sickness, requiring the use of antibiotics. This over use of antibiotics within our livestock will, over time, increase our resistance and lead to greater health risks within the human population.

FOR EXAMPLE

Organic free-range eggs provide us with the right ratio of Omega 3-6 essential fats that we need. Whereas intensively commercial farmed battery eggs can be 20:1 in the wrong direction!

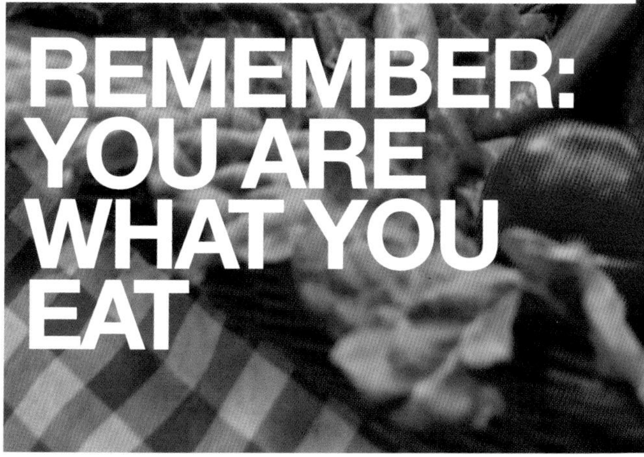

REMEMBER: YOU ARE WHAT YOU EAT

why detox?_

We call Phase 1 the detox phase for the simple reason that your body is cleansed from the toxins of both alcohol and sugar. This phase will really kick start the fat loss, helping you break the addiction of simple 'empty' carbohydrates and form regular eating patterns.

Non-dairy – Phase 1

Cow's dairy is one of the most common food intolerances. If you find yourself craving either milk or cheese, chances are you are sensitive.

Pasteurised milk increases the production of unhealthy mucus, which creates sinus and respiratory problems.

Due to the pasteurisation and homogenisation process the enzymes we need to digest milk are destroyed, creating possible lactose intolerance with symptoms ranging from abdominal bloating, gas, abdominal pains and diarrhea.

See alternatives in the protein section.

Before you detox:

Caution_

If any of the following applies to you, please seek advice from your GP before beginning Phase 1.

- You are pregnant
- You are breastfeeding
- You are taking any medications
- You are recovering from a serious illness
- You have just undergone any major surgery
- You are suffering from an eating disorder

phase 1_

"IT IS ABSOLUTELY INSANE NOT TO BE A HEALTH NUT"

Michael Murray, MD

Detox – Week 0-2

The Perfect Start

1. Strictly no alcohol
2. Strictly no caffeine
3. Strictly no sugar
4. Strictly no cow's dairy
5. Fruit is in shakes only
6. Eat every 3 hours – 5-6 small meals
7. Drink 0.033 x bodyweight in kg in water daily

Exercise 3 x week

Please refer to the workouts section for Phase 1 – gym or home-based.

Feel free to add in extra interval sessions.

phase 2_

"WE DON'T KNOW WHO WE ARE UNTIL WE SEE WHAT WE CAN DO"

Martha Grimes

Week 3-6
The Transition

The rules

1. 90/10 – You can cheat 10%
(This means 3 out of 35 weekly meals – inc alcohol e.g. sandwich – Monday lunchtime, chinese – Friday night, Sunday lunch and 1-2 alcoholic drinks)

2. 1-2 cups of tea/coffee (if desired) max before 2 pm

3. Lean protein, low GI carbs, healthy fats from the list at every meal

4. Eat every 3 hours – 5-6 meals

5. Drink 0.033 x bodyweight in kg in water daily

Exercise 3-4 x week

Please refer to the workouts section for Phase 2 – gym or home-based.

Once again you can add extra interval sessions in if desired.

phase 3_

"NEVER EAT MORE THAN YOU CAN LIFT"

Miss Piggy

top tip
If progress is halted, cut back daily kcals by 250 or reduce the amount of food at each meal.

NOTE: *Extra kcals allows you 10% more cheat time, however this does not mean you return to your old bad habits!*

REMEMBER:
NO 1 PRIORITY IS HEALTH!

Week 7-12 and onwards
From Here to Eternity

The rules

1. 20% cheating = up to 6 cheat meals or 3 cheats plus sensible alcohol allowance based on 35 correctly balanced meals.
2. 2-3 cups tea/coffee (if desired) max before 2 pm
3. Lean protein, low GI carbs, healthy fats from the list at every meal
4. Eat every 3-4 hours – 5-6 meals
5. Drink 0.033 x bodyweight in kg in water daily

Exercise 4 x week

Please refer to the workouts section for Phase 3 – gym or home-based.

cheat time_

The main focus for so many of you will be: How much? How often?

Remember the stricter you are, the sooner you will reach the goals you have set for yourself.

For more info please contact: MK Personal Training Academy 0870 442 7115

Phase 1

No cheating

Phase 2

10% cheating = 3 cheat meals out of 35 weekly

Phase 3

20% cheating = up to 6 cheat meals or 3 cheats plus sensible alcohol allowance based on 35 correctly balanced meals.

1 250ml glass of wine	= 1 cheat	**KEEP IT SIMPLE**
1 pint of beer	= 1 cheat	
1 dessert	= 1 cheat	

Because we know there will be times when you have extra cheats!

Extra cheat = exercise penalty 4 minute MK Lifefit Express workout.

YOUR GOALS MINUS YOUR DOUBTS EQUALS YOUR DREAMS

adidas

a word on Week 12_

(what now?)

So now you've completed the 12 weeks – a different person, what next?

The changes you have made have ensured success, but your journey to lasting health and vitality has only just started.

Remember your body can now adapt to the same exercise within 3-4 weeks and the structure of MK Lifefit is to prevent this. To continue your fantastic progress please refer to the **MK Personal Training Academy** website for more information.

www.mkpersonaltraining.co.uk

body fat_ the facts:

Your body composition i.e. the amount of you that is muscle, water and fat is far more important than your weight or BMI (Body Mass Index).

For far too long we have focused on weight and not the more important composition. When have you ever looked at someone on the beach and asked yourself how much they weigh?!

Either they are in good shape or bad shape and that is everything to do with how much body fat they are carrying.

Below are the ranges that we work with at **MK Personal Training Academy.**

To find out your body fat please contact: MK Personal Training Academy 0870 442 7115

MK Personal Training Academy goals:

	Average	Fit	Athletic
Men:	17% – 20%	14% – 17%	10% – 13%
Women:	24% – 27%	21% – 24%	16% – 20%

Note:

1 – 2 lbs of fat = 0.5% Body Fat

4 lbs of fat loss each month for 12 months = 12% body fat per year

12% body fat loss in 12 months could take you from obese to super fit... ***imagine that!***

WOMEN with waists over 35 inches:
Incredible high risk to health

MEN with waists over 40 inches:
Incredible high risk to health

WOMEN are borderline obese at 30%
Clinically obese at 35%

MEN are borderline obese at 25%
Clinically obese at 30%

Estrogen causes women to carry about 5% more fat then men.

monitoring your progress_

measurements

Take only 1 measurement a week at the same time of day, preferably morning.

weight: ______________________ hips: ______________________

waist: (around belly button) __________ thigh: ______________________

photographs: ***(at the start and the 12th week)***

body fat %: ***(please refer to MK Personal Training Academy)*** ____________

Allow 21 days for metabolism to shift to see if the plan is working.
Any problems please contact MK Personal Training Academy.

top tip
Workouts should be changed every 3-4 weeks to stop the body from adaption.

monitoring your progress_

your photos

To help you visually track your fitness progress, take photos of yourself at key stages within the 3 phases and stick them in the boxes provided below:

Phase 1 photo:

Phase 2 photo:

Phase 3 photo:

a word on food intolerance_

Are you someone who can't keep weight off no matter how strict you are?

You could be suffering from a hidden food allergy.

top tip
The Alcat test is a simple blood test to identify exactly which foods and chemicals are causing problems. Call us now on 0870 442 7115.

A tremendous amount of health problems have been linked to food intolerance – common everyday problems like migraines, aching joints, fatigue, gastro intestinal disorders, eczema, hyperactivity/ADD, asthma and obesity.

Your "trigger foods" can be as common as oranges or wheat and could be holding back the weight loss. By discovering and eliminating **those trigger foods you can lose weight and regain energy naturally.**

At **MK Personal Training Academy** we believe the only person who will look after your health and wellbeing is **you.**

We recommend a full health assessment every 12 months, to measure all aspects of health from kidney, liver and cardiovascular function to blood sugar, cholesterol and hormonal balance, alongside a full fitness assessment.

We need to change our thought process from existing with aches, pains, tiredness and the need for prescriptive drugs with side effects from time to time, to that of disease prevention and a long, healthy vitality full life.

exercise_

At **MK Personal Training Academy**, we believe everyone is unique. Exercise programs should be tailor made to the individual, based on their own body's needs and their individual goals.

We find, however, that the majority of people exercising, very rarely reach their goals and generally find themselves frustrated.

Exercise for fat loss is a science. It is based on creating something called Exercise Post Oxygen Consumption – EPOC, which causes the metabolism to be elevated for 36+ hours after training has finished. Burning huge amounts of fat after you have finished in the gym. Specific types of resistance training, combined with high intensity interval training, are the keys to creating EPOC.

Please refer to our website to gain access to the MK Lifefit fat loss programs after Week 12.

special considerations_

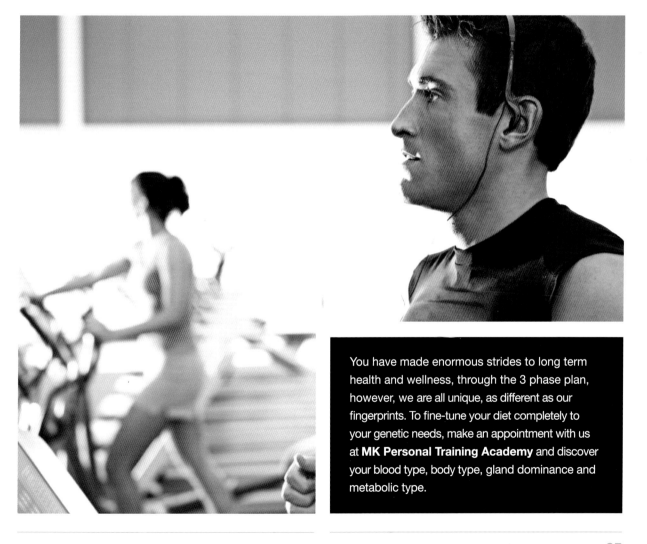

You have made enormous strides to long term health and wellness, through the 3 phase plan, however, we are all unique, as different as our fingerprints. To fine-tune your diet completely to your genetic needs, make an appointment with us at **MK Personal Training Academy** and discover your blood type, body type, gland dominance and metabolic type.

the time is now_

"I WANT TO LOOK GOOD NAKED"

Lester from the film American Beauty in answer to the question "Well are you just looking to lose weight, or do you want to have increased strength and flexibility as well"

We urgently need to change.

We supposedly know more now, than we ever have before. We are more advanced in technology and are achieving more in modern medicine than we ever dreamed possible. However, statistics prove we have as much, if not more, disease now than ever, not as a result of poor sanitation and hygiene, as in the past, but very much to do with malnutrition.

We have an obesity epidemic, in a low fat obsessed society and signs only show the situation deteriorating.

DESIRE to change above anything is needed to empower us to take responsibility for our own health and wellbeing.

Prevention is better than cure. Through exercise, proper whole food nutrition and natural health products, we can positively influence our genetics greater than we thought possible. We now need to combine all 3 aspects together, rather than following one in isolation, to not only stay clear of pain and inflammation but to actually feel real energy and vitality everyday.

So what are you waiting for?

THE RECIPE SECTION_

Gareth Cole, former head chef of the Crabmill, Clavedon and now head chef and joint owner of the Hurdles, Droxford.

Gareth worked with Matt to create the innovative and delicious menus contained in this book, with the primary focus on health.

phase 1_
detox 14 days:

Breakfast_

MK morning shake

- 1 cup 250 ml freshly squeezed grapefruit/orange or 1/2 cup of berries fresh/frozen
- 2 scoops of whey protein
- 1 tbsp Flax oil

Remember – you can change any ingredient for a likewise off 'Your Shopping List' (page 25).

Vegetarians – you can substitute meat or fish for tofu or quorn.

Note – all recipe amounts can be slightly adjusted to suit the individual.

Snacks_
mid morning and mid afternoon

Choice of small tin tuna/ salmon/mackerel

Protein shake

Mixed nuts (10)

Celery sticks (2) with natural peanut butter dip

Hard boiled eggs (2-3)

Lunches_

Spinach salad

- 2 bags baby spinach or 4 bunches fresh spinach leaves
- 1/2 lb (225g) button mushrooms
- Handful of chopped spring onion
- 3 hard boiled eggs
- 1/2 cup (125 ml) goat feta cheese
- Tracy Holly salad dressing

Wash dry and trim stems of spinach leaves. Cut leaves in half with sharp knife, add to large salad bowl. Add clean and thinly sliced mushrooms to salad bowl. Cube feta, chop onion and eggs and add to salad bowl. Cover and refrigerate all ingredients till ready to serve. Add dressing and toss. Season with crushed black pepper.

To add more protein cook in 6oz of chicken as required.

MAKES 6 LARGE SERVINGS

PER SERVING

Calories	Protein	Carbohydrates	Fat
151	12.6g	11g	6.4g

With thanks to Tracy Holly

Chicken and avocado salad

- 2 handfuls of mixed green leaves (spinach, rocket, watercress, lettuce)
- 4oz chicken (cooked)
- 2oz cherry tomatoes
- 10oz alfalfa sprouts
- 2 tbsp pitted olives (green or black)
- 1/2 avocado

Dressing

- 1/2 clove garlic
- Pinch of dried chilli
- 3 tbsp lemon juice
- 1 tbsp olive oil
- 55g (2oz) almonds

THE DRESSING SERVES 2

PER SERVING

Calories	Protein	Carbohydrates	Fat
242	6g	7g	21g

Put the mixed green leaves, chicken, tomatoes, alfalfa sprouts and pitted olives into a serving dish. Scoop out and add the avocado flesh. Crush the garlic and put in a bowl or screw-top jar along with the dried chilli, lemon juice and olive oil. Give it a good mix or shake and pour over the salad. Give the salad a good toss so the ingredients are covered with the oil. Finally, crush the almonds so they are ground into little bits – you can do this by putting them in a little plastic bag and crushing with a rolling pin. Sprinkle the nuts over the salad and enjoy.

SERVES 2

PER SERVING

Calories	Protein	Carbohydrates	Fat
272	25.5g	15.6g	12g

With thanks to Tracy Holly

Dressed red salmon salad with orange and basil

- 200g fresh red salmon (cooked) (tinned optional)
- 1 x tbsp light mayonnaise
- 1 x lemon (zest and juiced)
- 1 x lime (zest and juiced)
- 1 x bunch of spring onion (chopped)
- 1 x bunch basil (chopped)
- 1 x tbsp parsley (chopped)
- 2 x shots of Everyday Dressing
- 1 x tbsp of natural yoghurt
- 1 x orange (zest and juiced)
- 1 x tbsp olive oil
- Salt and pepper

Mix all ingredients in a bowl together, serve with fresh green salad.

SERVES 2 – COOKING TIME 15 MINUTES

PER SERVING

Calories	Protein	Carbohydrates	Fat
320	24.3g	20.5g	15.7g

Roasted tuna, red peppers with rocket salad

- 2 x large red peppers
- 1 x 200g tin of tuna (drained)
- 2 x large tomatoes (chopped and deseeded)
- 1 x tsp light mayonnaise
- 2 x spring onions (chopped)
- Salt and pepper
- 1 x bunch basil

Cut peppers in half and cut out seeds and core, mix tuna with mayonnaise, spring onion, chopped tomatoes and basil, add salt and pepper if required. Place back into peppers and bake in medium oven for 10-15 minutes until soft.

SERVES 2 – COOKING TIME 15 MINUTES

PER SERVING

Calories	Protein	Carbohydrates	Fat
225	29g	18.4g	4g

Grilled chicken with greek salad

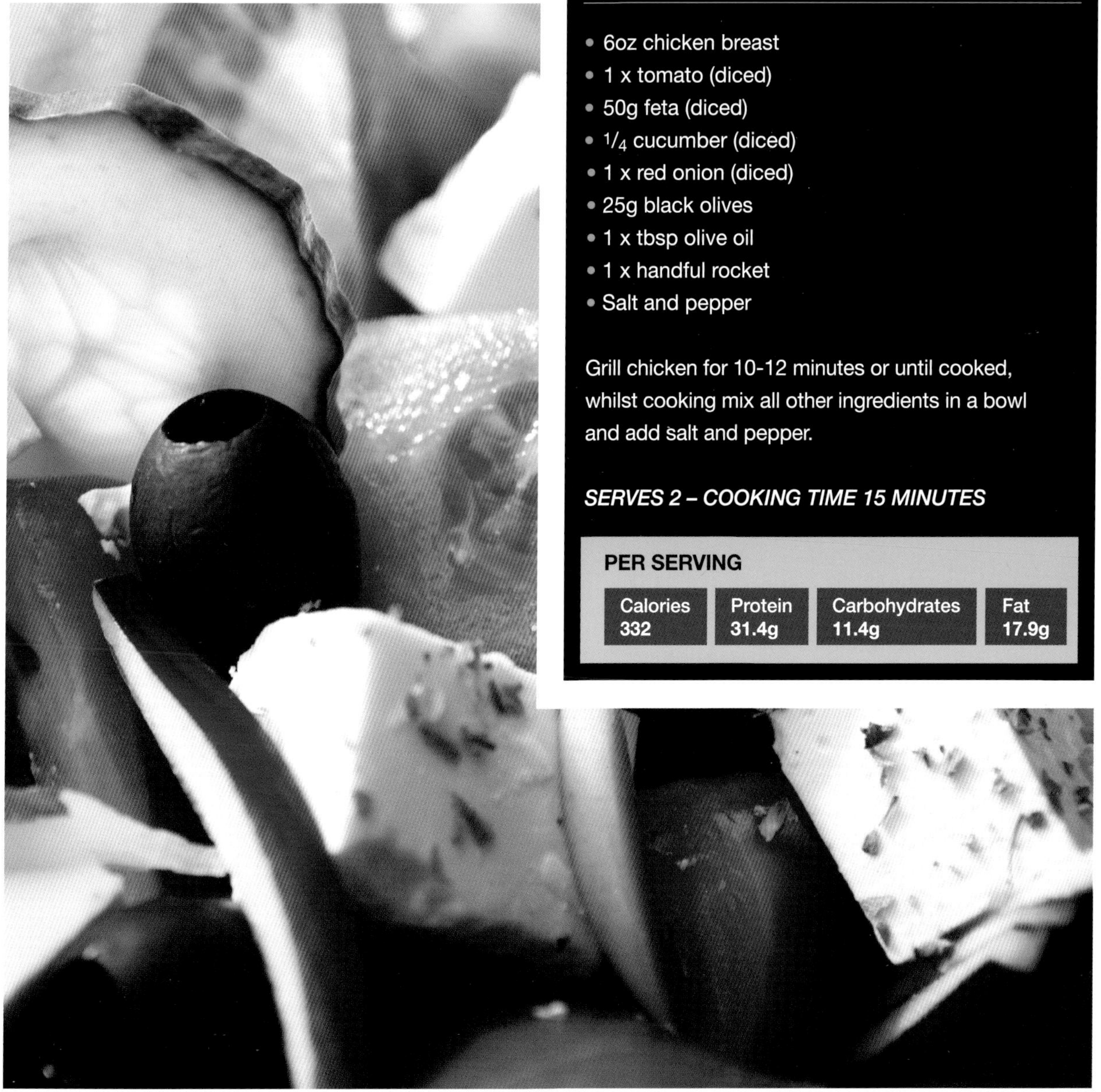

- 6oz chicken breast
- 1 x tomato (diced)
- 50g feta (diced)
- $^1/_4$ cucumber (diced)
- 1 x red onion (diced)
- 25g black olives
- 1 x tbsp olive oil
- 1 x handful rocket
- Salt and pepper

Grill chicken for 10-12 minutes or until cooked, whilst cooking mix all other ingredients in a bowl and add salt and pepper.

SERVES 2 – COOKING TIME 15 MINUTES

PER SERVING

Calories	Protein	Carbohydrates	Fat
332	31.4g	11.4g	17.9g

Dinners_

Thai marinated chicken kebabs with asian coleslaw

- 2 x kebab sticks
- 5oz skinned and boned chicken breast (diced in 2cm squares)
- 1 x lime
- 1 x bunch of coriander (chopped)
- 1 x tbsp of green thai pastes
- 1 x bunch of spring onion (chopped)
- 1 x carrot (grated)
- 1 x mouli (grated)
- 1 x red onion (sliced)
- 1 x tsp light mayonnaise
- 1 x tbsp olive oil

Put chicken cubes in a bowl with zest (grated) lime, 1 tsp of thai paste and half of the chopped coriander, mix round with olive oil until well covered, skewer chicken pieces on kebab sticks, cook under baltan or grill for 10-15 minutes, or until cooked. (If you soak the kebab sticks in cold water before grilling you will prevent them from burning) In a separate bowl, mix juice of lime, with all other ingredients to form Asian coleslaw.

SERVES 2 – COOKING TIME 20-25 MINUTES (can be stored in refrigerator for up to 3 days)

PER SERVING

Calories	Protein	Carbohydrates	Fat
260	23.8g	14.7g	11.8g

Warm lentil salad with boiled egg and gratin tomatoes

- 200g puy lentils
- 1 x pint vegetable stock
- 1 x tbsp olive oil
- 1 x red onion (sliced)
- 2 x fresh plum tomatoes
- 1 x bunch of chives (chopped)
- 2 x free range eggs (boiled)
- 1 x packet of green beans
- 1 x bag of rocket
- 2 x tbsp of lemon juice
- Salt and pepper
- 1 x tbsp cumin powder

Place lentils in a saucepan with veg stock and bring to the boil and simmer for 15 minutes until soft, add more stock if needed, place two halved tomatoes under grill with olive oil and salt and pepper, cook for 5 minutes until soft, cool lentils down under warm water, mix cumin powder, herbs and onion, add other ingredients and serve.

SERVES 2 – COOKING TIME 25 MINUTES

PER SERVING

Calories	Protein	Carbohydrates	Fat
359	19.4g	41.6g	12.9g

Seared peppered tuna steak with green salad and hummus

- 300g fresh tuna steaks
- 1 x tbsp coarse ground black pepper
- 2 x tomatoes (seeded and diced)
- 1/2 cucumber (diced)
- 1/2 x jar pitted black olives (50g)
- 50g feta cheese (diced)
- 100g hummus
- 1 x tbsp olive oil
- Rocket (optional)

Roll tuna in olive oil and sprinkle the black pepper over it to stick. Heat a frying pan with a little oil and fry tuna for 3-4 minutes each side on a medium heat, mix all diced salads together with rocket and olive oil, serve tuna on top of salad and spoon hummus over the tuna steak.

SERVES 2 – COOKING TIME 15-20 MINUTES

PER SERVING

Calories	Protein	Carbohydrates	Fat
469	44.5g	19.7g	23.7g

Salmon stir fry

- 200g salmon (cooked)
- 110g mange tout (sliced)
- 1 x red pepper (seared and sliced)
- 100g mushrooms (sliced)
- 100g bean sprouts
- 1/2 bunch coriander
- 1/2 red onion (sliced)
- 1 x tsp pickled ginger
- 2 x tbsp soy sauce
- 1 x tbsp sesame oil
- 1 x zest and juice of lime
- 1 x garlic clove (chopped)

Heat oil in large wok, fry onions and peppers for 1-2 minutes, add mange tout, mushrooms and bean sprouts and cook for a further 2 minutes. Add salmon and garlic and cook for a further 2 minutes. Add ginger, coriander, lime, sesame oil and soy sauce and fry for a further 2 minutes.

SERVES 2 – COOKING TIME 15 MINUTES

PER SERVING

Calories	Protein	Carbohydrates	Fat
303	31.9g	17.4g	11.8g

Moroccan turkey with raw vegetable salad

- 2 x 100g turkey fillet
- 1 x tbsp olive oil
- 1 x carrot (diced)
- 1/4 cucumber (diced)
- 1 x red pepper (slice thin)
- 1 x red chilli (finely chopped)
- 1 x tsp paprika
- 1/4 tbsp cinnamon powder
- 1 x bunch mint
- 1 x red onion (finely diced)
- 1 x lemon (zest and juiced)
- Salt and pepper

Peel the carrot and cucumber, discard the skin and dice. Mix with red onions, pepper and mint. Add lemon and olive oil and season with salt and pepper. To create salad, baton out the turkey to create thin fillet. Rub with spices and chilli, add a little olive oil and grill for 10 minutes and serve with salad.

SERVES 2 – COOKING TIME 25 MINUTES

PER SERVING

Calories	Protein	Carbohydrates	Fat
294	32g	17.9g	10.5g

phase 2/3_recipes:

Breakfasts_

Protein oatmeal

- 1 cup rolled oats
- 1 cup rice/soya milk or 4 cups water
- 1 scoop of whey protein
- 1/2 cup fresh/frozen blueberries or raspberries
- 1 tsp cinnamon
- Sweeten with manuka honey
- Optional add – raw nuts (almonds etc) or raw seeds (flax, sunflower etc)

Boil in a saucepan or if short on time, microwave for 1 minute, stir and then microwave for a further minute.

SERVES 2

PER SERVING

Calories	Protein	Carbohydrates	Fat
286	15.5g	44.7g	5g

Protein blueberry pancakes

- 2 cups wholewheat pancake mix (preferably buckwheat)
- 2 scoops whey protein
- 1 cup (250ml) filtered water
- 4 whole eggs
- 1 tsp vanilla extract
- 1 cup fresh/frozen blueberries
- 1 medium banana

In a blender add water, protein powder, eggs, vanilla, berries and banana and process until smooth. In a skillet or frying pan, add large scoop of mixture on a low heat and flip over after small bubbles appear (about 5 minutes).

SERVES 8

PER SERVING

Calories	Protein	Carbohydrates	Fat
128	9.5g	13.7g	4g

Muesli

- 2 cups rolled oats
- 4 tbsp whole flax seeds
- 1/2 cup oat bran
- 1/4 cup wheat bran
- 1/4 cup sliced almonds
- 1/4 cup perfect sweet (Xylitol)
- 1 tsp coconut extract

Stir all ingredients into a mixing bowl. Spread out the muesli into a baking dish coated with olive oil. Bake at 300 degrees F, for approximately 40 minutes. After cooling add rice milk and a handful of mixed nuts and seeds. Manuka honey to taste if required.

SERVES 10

PER SERVING

Calories	Protein	Carbohydrates	Fat
115	4.1g	16.3g	3.8g

Omelettes with additions

- 3 egg whites plus 1 whole egg
- Choice of – handful of spinach, onion, mushrooms, feta cheese, tomato or peppers

Cook on a low heat and then place under a grill to finish off.

SERVES 1

PER SERVING *(Not Including Additions)*

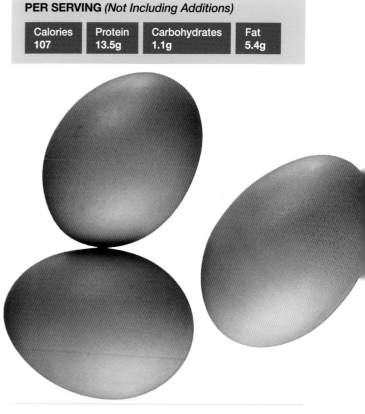

Calories	Protein	Carbohydrates	Fat
107	13.5g	1.1g	5.4g

Lunches_

Pear, spinach and walnut salad with cottage cheese

- 2 x fresh ripe pears
- 1 x bag baby spinach (2 x bunches)
- 50g walnuts
- 100g cottage cheese
- 2 x spring onions (sliced)
- 1 x tbsp olive oil
- 1 x tsp lemon juice
- Salt and pepper

Mix all ingredients in a bowl together and serve with cottage cheese on top.

SERVES 2 – COOKING TIME 15 MINUTES

PER SERVING

Calories	Protein	Carbohydrates	Fat
491	21g	44g	25.6g

Smoked haddock and spinach omelette

- 100g smoked haddock (cooked and shredded)
- 100g spinach (cooked)
- 3 x free range eggs (1 yolk)
- 1 x tbsp olive oil
- $1/2$ x red onion

Heat a large non-stick pan with olive oil. Whisk eggs together with salt and pepper. Add to pan and move around with fork. Add smoked haddock, red onion and spinach. Once eggs are set, fold over and serve.

SERVES 1 – COOKING TIME 10 MINUTES

PER SERVING

Calories	Protein	Carbohydrates	Fat
385	41g	10.3g	20g

Grilled mackerel with spicy brown rice

- 2 x mackerel fillets (unsmoked)
- 1 x red onion
- 1 x bunch coriander (chopped)
- 1 x lemon (zest and juiced)
- 1 x tbsp olive oil
- 50g brown rice
- 1 x red pepper (sliced)

Rub mackerel fillets with olive oil and grill for 3-4 minutes each side until cooked. Boil rice for 12-15 minutes, then drain well. Fry onions and red pepper for 3 minutes, add rice, lemon and coriander. Season with salt and pepper and serve.

SERVES 2 – COOKING TIME 15 MINUTES

PER SERVING

Calories	Protein	Carbohydrates	Fat
376	23g	19g	23g

Easy tuna gazpachio

- 1 x tin 400g chopped tomatoes
- 1 x red onion (chopped)
- $^{1}/_{3}$ cucumber (chopped)
- 1 tbsp lemon juice
- 2 x sprigs of mint (chopped finely)
- 1 x sprig of parsley (chopped finely)
- 1 x red pepper (chopped)
- 1 x tbsp olive oil
- 1 x 180g tinned tuna (drained)
- 2 x spring onions (sliced)
- 1 x fresh green chilli (chopped)

Mix all ingredients in a high powered blender except for herbs and spring onion and tuna, blend to smooth puree. Pour into a bowl with tuna, spring onions and herbs, season with salt and pepper, served chilled.

SERVES 1-2 – COOKING TIME 10 MINUTES

PER SERVING

Calories	Protein	Carbohydrates	Fat
290	23g	28.6g	8g

Smoked salmon and fresh herb scrambled eggs with green salad

- 150g of smoked salmon (sliced)
- 4 x free range eggs (beaten)
- 1 x bunch parsley (chopped)
- 1 x sprig of dill (chopped)
- 1 x bag of mixed salad leaves
- Multigrain or rye bread
- Salt and pepper
- 1 x tsp olive oil

Heat oil in a large saucepan, add eggs and cook over low heat, stirring constantly to prevent eggs sticking, when cooked add herbs and smoked salmon and serve on toasted multigrain/rye bread.
Serve with mixed salad leaves dressed with olive oil.

SERVES 2 – COOKING TIME 10-15 MINUTES

PER SERVING

Calories	Protein	Carbohydrates	Fat
347	27g	18g	18.6g

Roast pumpkin salad with basil, watercress, pine nuts and cottage cheese

- 200g fresh pumpkin
- 1 x bunch of basil (chopped)
- 1 x bunch of watercress
- 1 x tbsp of pine nuts
- 100g Cottage cheese
- 1 x red onion (sliced)
- 2 x tbsp lemon juice
- 1 x tbsp olive oil
- 2 x tsp paprika
- Salt and pepper

Dice pumpkin into 2 cm cubes; mix it in a bowl with half of the chopped Basil, Paprika, and Olive oil, and cook on medium heat for 10 minutes, or until soft. Add lemon juices to watercress, slice red onion and pine nuts in bowl, mix in pumpkin, serve with cottage cheese on top.

SERVES 2 – COOKING TIME 15 MINUTES

PER SERVING

Calories	Protein	Carbohydrates	Fat
221	10g	15.5g	13.2g

Chicken caesar salad

- 6oz chicken fillet
- 1 x tbsp olive oil
- 1 x garlic clove (finely chopped)
- 1 x large head little gems or cos lettuce
- 1 x slice of rye bread or seeded bread (toasted and cubed)
- 2 x spring onions (sliced)
- 2 x tbsp light mayonnaise
- 1 x tbsp water
- 2 x tbsp lemon juice
- 2 x anchovy fillets

For the dressing, mix mayonnaise, water lemon juice and anchovies in blender and puree. Toss the rest of the ingredients round in a salad bowl and add dressing and gently mix through and serve with chicken. Dressing can be kept for 4-5 days.

SERVES 2 – COOKING TIME 15 MINUTES

PER SERVING

Calories	Protein	Carbohydrates	Fat
359	33.5g	19g	16.5g

Dinners_

Grilled cod with sesame spinach and spicy tomato vinegarette

- 2 (4oz) cod fillets
- 1 x bag of spinach
- 1 x tsp sesame seeds
- 2 x shots of Tabasco sauce
- 2 x shots of Worcester sauce
- 1 x tsp dijon mustard
- 2 x tbsp lemon juice
- 2 x tbsp olive oil
- Salt and pepper

Grill cod under bottom of grill for 10 minutes with drizzle of olive oil, whilst cooking put spinach in saucepan with a touch of water and sesame seeds, cook for 5 minutes until wilted down, drain off water, then season with salt and pepper. In separate bowl, mix all other ingredients with whisk to form vinaigrette, serve immediately, add more Tabasco for extra spice.

SERVES 2 – COOKING TIME 25 MINUTES

PER SERVING

Calories	Protein	Carbohydrates	Fat
321	31.9g	12.6g	15.9g

Aromatic steamed sea bass

- 1-2 fillets sea bass
- 1 x leek (fine strips)
- 1 x bag spinach
- 1 x carrot (fine strips)
- 1 x lemongrass (chopped roughly)
- 1 x bunch ginger (chopped roughly)
- 2 x sprigs rosemary
- 1 x sprig thyme
- 1 x clove garlic
- 1 x lime

Place carrots, leeks and spinach on A4 size piece of baking paper turned on the side, put herbs on top of vegetables, place sea bass on top and gently score the skin opening up the flesh slightly, stuff ginger, garlic and lemon grass into pockets In fish skin, place herbs on top. Squeeze lime on top and add 2 tablespoons of water, fold paper in half with fish at bottom, pinch bottom ends and roll top forming a sealed bag, bake in oven for 20 -25 minutes at 200 degrees C.

SERVES 2 – COOKING TIME 35 MINUTES

PER SERVING

Calories	Protein	Carbohydrates	Fat
274	35g	24g	4.2g

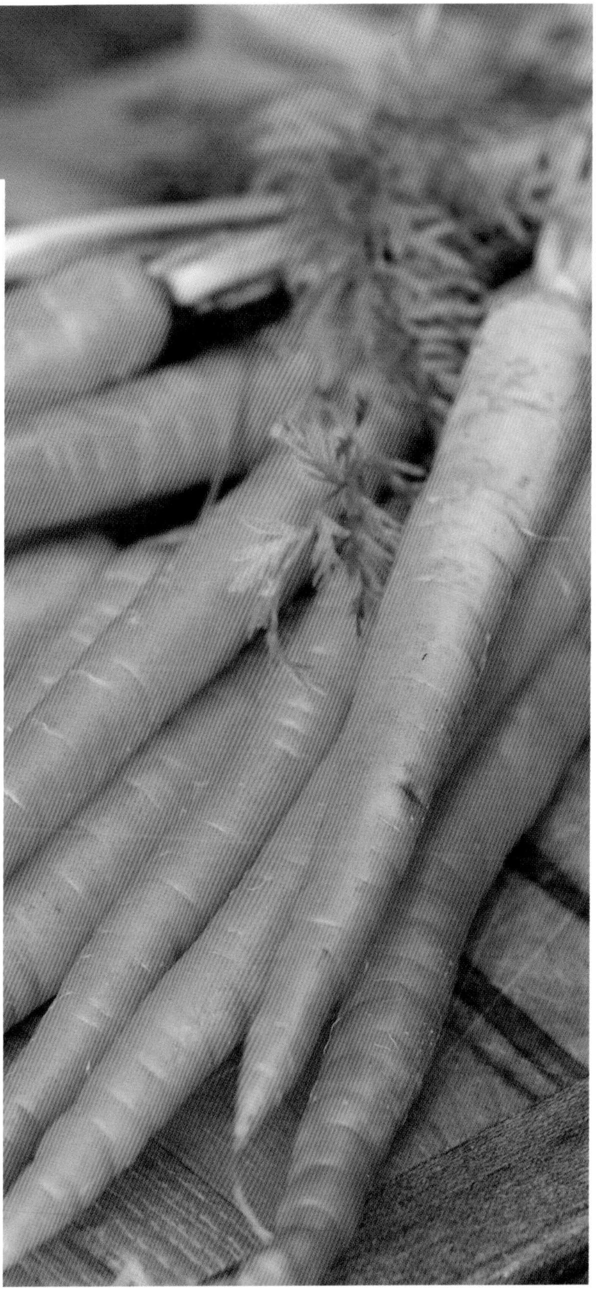

Tuna kebab with stir fry vegetables and hummus

- 1 x 180g fresh tuna (2cm chunks)
- 1 x red pepper (sliced)
- 1 x bag of bean sprouts
- 1 x onion (sliced)
- 1 x carrot (sliced)
- 1 x bag mange tout (sliced)
- 1 x 100g tub hummus
- 2 x kebab sticks
- 1 x bunch basil (chopped)
- 1 x clove garlic (sliced)
- 1 x bunch coriander
- 1 x tbsp olive oil

Skewer tuna chunks onto kebab sticks about 6 chunks on each kebab if possible. Rub in olive oil first, add salt and pepper and grill for 10 minutes. In large pan heat olive oil to smoking hot, add all sliced veg and fry for 5 minutes until soft, add coriander at the end and serve with hummus.

SERVES 2

PER SERVING

Calories	Protein	Carbohydrates	Fat
387	31.7g	35.7g	13g

Italian chicken with sweet potato rosti

- 3oz chicken breast
- 1 x sprig basil (chopped)
- 1 x garlic clove (chopped)
- 1 x lemon (zest and juiced)
- 1 x sweet potato (grated)
- 1 x maris piper or desiree potato (grated)
- 200g spinach
- 1 x egg yolk
- Salt and pepper

Mix chicken breast in a bowl with basil, garlic and lemon, add a touch of olive oil and cook in oven for 15 minutes or until cooked. Mix potatoes in a bowl with egg yolk to form a stiff mix, fry in frying pan, 1-2 cm thick, for 2-3 minutes each side and then in a low to medium oven for a further 5 minutes. Boil spinach in boiling water for 3 minutes, drain well add salt and pepper and serve all together.

SERVES 1-2 – COOKING TIME 25 MINUTES

PER SERVING

Calories	Protein	Carbohydrates	Fat
266	21g	36g	4.4g

Grilled fillet steak salad with marinated mushroom and mustard dressing

- 1 x 100g fillet steak (flattened out)
- 100g button mushrooms (sliced or whole)
- 1 x red onion (sliced)
- 1 x tbsp olive oil
- 1 x tsp wholegrain mustard
- 1 x bag mixed salad leaves
- 1 x tsp white wine vinegar
- 1 x bunch parsley (chopped)
- 1/2 bag mange tout (sliced thin)

Fry sliced mushrooms in olive oil for 2 minutes and mix with vinegar, parsley, mange tout, salt and pepper. Leave for 5 minutes and cover with cling film. Grill steak for 2-3 minutes each side, once cooked, slice thinly and add to mushrooms. Add olive oil and mustard and leave for a further 3 minutes, once warm mix in leaves and serve.

SERVES 1

PER SERVING

Calories	Protein	Carbohydrates	Fat
432	28g	26.4g	24g

Grilled salmon fillet with stir fry lime and ginger, vegetables and mint yoghurt

- 2 x salmon fillets (skinned)
- 100g bean sprouts
- 100g mange tout (sliced)
- 1 x red pepper (sliced)
- 1 x bunch coriander
- 1 x carrot (thinly sliced)
- 1 x lime (zest and juiced)
- 1 x tbsp ginger (chopped)
- 1 x sprig mint
- 1 x tbsp greek yoghurt
- 1 x head broccoli (chopped)

In a hot wok, fry all the vegetables together for 5 minutes; add the lime, ginger and coriander at the end when vegetables are cooked. Grill salmon fillets with olive oil for 4-5 minutes each side until cooked. Then mix mint and yoghurt together and serve on top of salmon once cooked.

SERVES 2 – COOKING TIME 20 MINUTES

PER SERVING

Calories	Protein	Carbohydrates	Fat
301	29g	26g	9g

Smoked chicken and spicy quinoa with grilled vegetables

- 1 x pint chicken stock
- 150g chicken (smoked)
- 100g quinoa
- 1 x courgette (diced)
- 1 x aubergine (diced)
- 1 x red pepper (diced)
- 1 x red onion (diced)
- 1 x bunch basil (chopped)
- 1 x red chilli (finely chopped)
- 1 x tsp paprika
- 1 x tbsp olive oil
- 1 x garlic clove (chopped)

Roast all vegetables with garlic, olive oil and basil in a hot oven for 10-15 minutes. Pour boiling chicken stock over cooked quinoa and leave for 5 minutes with cling film covering. Add paprika and chilli to quinoa and mix chicken through, serve roasted vegetables on the side.

SERVES 2 – COOKING TIME 25 MINUTES

PER SERVING

Calories	Protein	Carbohydrates	Fat
323	31g	25g	11g

Soups_

Tuna and white bean soup with chilli and basil

- 1 x 180g canned tuna in spring water, drained and broken into chunks
- 1 x 250g can of white beans (cannellini beans) (drained)
- 1 x large red chilli, chopped small
- 1 x bunch of basil, chopped or ripped
- 1 x onion chopped
- 1 x 400g chopped tomatoes
- 1/2 pint of vegetable stock
- 1 x bunch of spring onion (chopped)
- Salt and pepper
- 1 x tbsp of olive oil

Heat olive oil in a saucepan, add onions, and cook gently over medium heat for about 5 minutes until soft. Add chopped chilli, vegetable stock and chopped tomatoes, bring to boil and simmer for further 2 minutes, add basil directly before serving. Add additional chilli paste if you wish for extra flavour or heat, also you could serve with a greed salad.

SERVES 2 – COOKING TIME 15 MINUTES

PER SERVING

Calories	Protein	Carbohydrates	Fat
460	31g	51g	14.7g

Smoked haddock and watercress soup

- 2 x bunch of watercress
- 1 x bag of loose spinach
- 1 x bunch of parsley (chopped)
- 1 1/2 pints x vegetable stock
- 1 x fillet skinned smoked haddock (chopped)
- 1 x lemon
- Salt and pepper
- 1 x onion (roughly chopped)
- 1 x clove garlic (roughly chopped)
- 1 x tsp dijon mustard

Cook onions and garlic in saucepan for 5 minutes until soft, add stock, parsley spinach and watercress, bring back to the boil, put all ingredients except the smoked haddock into the blender and blend thoroughly to make smooth soup, return to saucepan, add smoked haddock and poach for further 5 minutes, add mustard and lemon.

SERVES 2 – COOKING TIME 15 MINUTES

PER SERVING

Calories	Protein	Carbohydrates	Fat
242	31g	25g	2g

Chicken, spinach and mushroom soup

- 3oz chicken breast (diced)
- 1 x 200g bag of button mushrooms (sliced)
- 1 x bag frozen sweet corn
- 1 x bag fresh spinach
- 1 1/2 pints chicken stock
- 1 x bunch spring onion (chopped)

Place sliced mushrooms in a saucepan and cook over medium heat for 2-3 minutes. Add diced chicken and cook for further 5 minutes until cooked, pour in stock and simmer with spinach and sweet corn for further 5 minutes, add chopped spring onions.

SERVES 2 – COOKING TIME 15 MINUTES

PER SERVING

Calories	Protein	Carbohydrates	Fat
352	34g	45g	4g

Sweet potato, basil and chicken soup

- 2 x medium sweet potatoes (diced small)
- 4oz chicken breast (Skinned and chopped small)
- 1 x onion (chopped)
- 1 x 1 1/2 pints of chicken stock
- 1 x bay leaf
- 1 x clove garlic
- 1 x bunch of basil
- 1 x leek (optional)
- 1 x tbspn olive oil

Cook onion, garlic and leeks in a saucepan on medium heat for 5 minutes until soft, add stock, bay leaf, chicken and sweet potato and simmer for 10 minutes until cooked. (make sure the sweet potato and chicken are same size). Add basil directly before serving with salt and pepper. (This is more of a broth soup, so does not require blending).

SERVES 2 – COOKING TIME 15-20 MINUTES

PER SERVING

Calories	Protein	Carbohydrates	Fat
335	25g	38.5g	9g

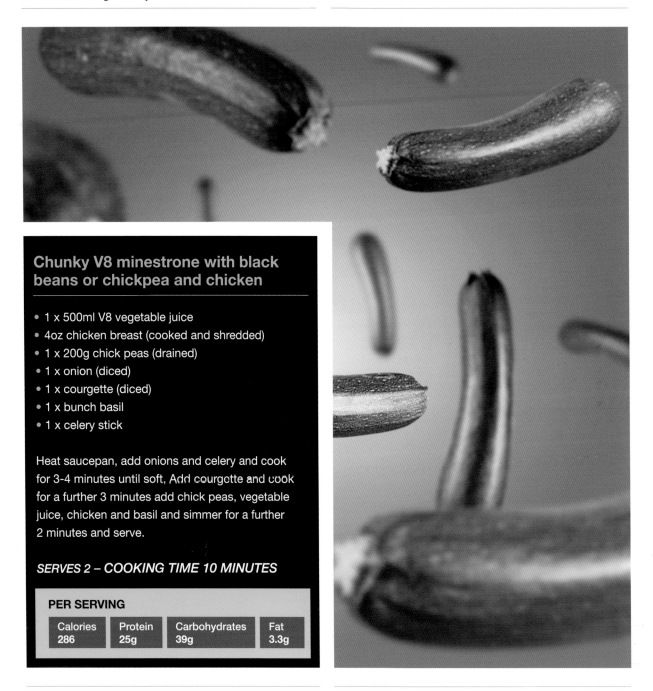

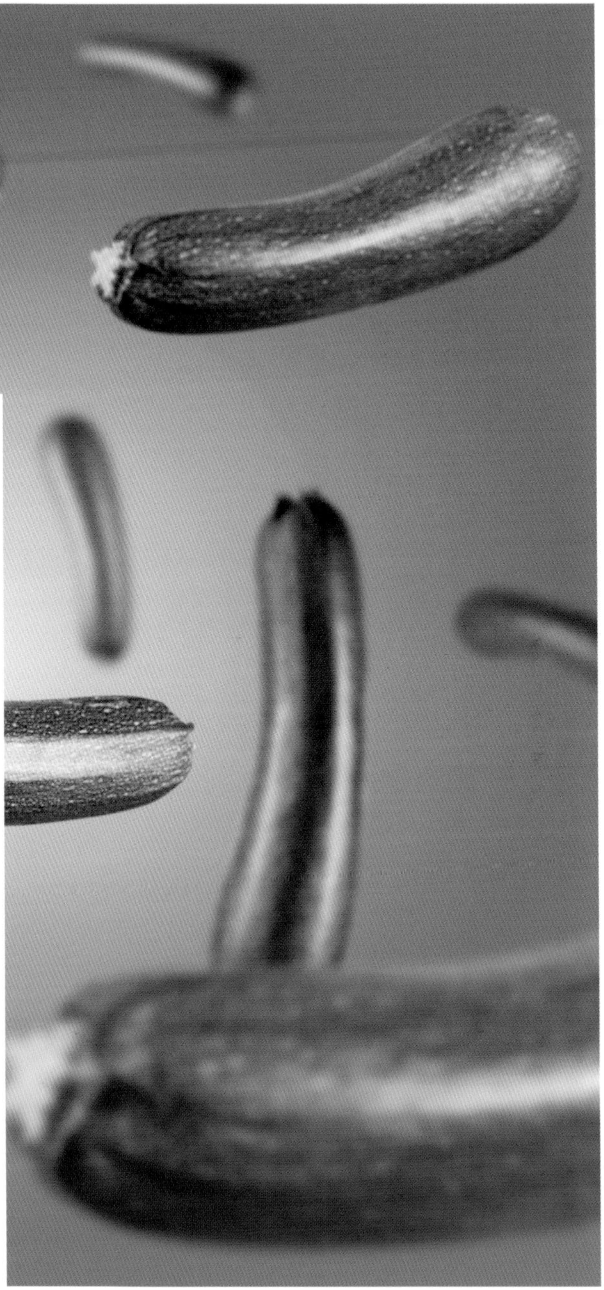

Chunky V8 minestrone with black beans or chickpea and chicken

- 1 x 500ml V8 vegetable juice
- 4oz chicken breast (cooked and shredded)
- 1 x 200g chick peas (drained)
- 1 x onion (diced)
- 1 x courgette (diced)
- 1 x bunch basil
- 1 x celery stick

Heat saucepan, add onions and celery and cook for 3-4 minutes until soft. Add courgette and cook for a further 3 minutes add chick peas, vegetable juice, chicken and basil and simmer for a further 2 minutes and serve.

SERVES 2 – COOKING TIME 10 MINUTES

PER SERVING

Calories	Protein	Carbohydrates	Fat
286	25g	39g	3.3g

1 small tin tuna, salmon, or mackerel

Hard boiled eggs (1-2)

N.B; these should not be boiled – simmer in water. Cover eggs in cold water, bring to the boil then remove from heat and leave covered in water with lid for a further 15 minutes.

Protein shake – see recipes

Plain mixed seeds and nuts – 10 (large handful)

Celery with natural peanut butter dip

4 Nut bar

Mixed spice crunch bar

Cranberry and raisin flapjack

Apricot snack bar

4 nut bar

- 50g pecans
- 50g almonds
- 50g hazel nuts
- 25g walnut pieces
- 2 whole omega 3 or free range eggs
- 2 egg whites (beaten)
- 6 scoops of vanilla whey powder
- 10g perfect sweet
- 1 tbsp olive oil
- 1 tbsp orange juice

Process the pecan, almond and hazel nuts together in a food blender. Mix all ingredients together until thoroughly mixed. Spread the mixture into a 8 x 8 baking tin that has been sprayed with olive oil. Bake a 350 degrees F for 12-15 minutes.

MAKES 12 PORTIONS

PER SERVING

Calories	Protein	Carbohydrates	Fat
144	9g	2.3g	11g

Mixed spice crunch bar

- 100g rolled oats
- 6 scoops of vanilla whey powder
- 50g raisins
- 2 cooking apples (stewed unsweetened)
- 1 tbsp olive oil
- 2 tsp mixed spice
- 1 tsp vanilla flavouring
- $^1/_2$ tsp perfect sweet

Process 50g of the rolled oats into flour in a food blender. Stir together the oat flour, the other 50g rolled oats, raisins, and protein powder in a mixing bowl. Add the sweetener, olive oil, vanilla flavouring, mixed spice and the stewed apple. Mix thoroughly. Spray an 8 x 8 inch baking tin with olive oil and spread mixture evenly into the tin. Bake at 200 degrees F for 12-15 minutes.

MAKES 8-10 PORTIONS

PER SERVING

Calories	Protein	Carbohydrates	Fat
120	7.4g	16.8g	2.6g

Cranberry and raisin flapjack

- 75g rolled oats
- 50g rolled oats blended
- 5 scoops chocolate whey powder
- 10g perfect sweet
- 25g dried cranberries
- 25g dried raisins
- 1 tsp baking powder
- 1 tsp cinnamon
- 2 tbsp honey
- 1 tbsp olive oil
- 1 cooking apple (stewed unsweetened)

Mix together all the dry ingredients in a food processor, slowly add the honey, apple and oil on a low speed until thoroughly mixed. Pour the mixture into an 8 x 9 inch baking tin sprayed with olive oil. Bake for 10-12 minutes 200 degrees F.

MAKES 10-12 PORTIONS

PER SERVING

Calories	Protein	Carbohydrates	Fat
101	6g	14.5g	2.2g

Apricot snack bar

- 125g Apricots (chopped)
- 5 scoops chocolate whey powder
- 100g rolled oats
- 10g cocoa powder (unsweetened)
- 10g perfect sweet
- 2 cooking apples (stewed unsweetened)

Mix 50g of the oats into flour in a food blender, mix all dry ingredients together. Add the apple and apricots 1 tbsp at a time, trying to use as little as possible not making the mixture too wet. Spread into an 8 x 8 baking tin sprayed with olive oil. Bake for 15 – 20 minutes.

MAKES 10-12 PORTIONS

PER SERVING

Calories	Protein	Carbohydrates	Fat
101	6g	17g	1.1g

Shakes_

Just add a blender!

Berry bonanza

- 1-2 scoops of whey protein
- 1 cup of fresh/frozen strawberries
- $^1/_2$ cup fresh/frozen blueberries
- 1 cup of ice (optional)
- 250ml water

Calories	Protein	Carbohydrates	Fat
193	21.5g	22.5g	1.9g

Flax fantastic

- 1-2 scoops whey protein
- 2 tbsps flax seeds
- $^1/_3$ cup cottage cheese
- $^1/_2$oz of almonds
- 1 cup of ice (optional)
- 250ml water

Calories	Protein	Carbohydrates	Fat
322	37.7g	11.8g	15.1g

Banana and walnut

- 1-2 scoops whey protein
- 1 banana
- 1oz walnuts
- 1 cup of ice (optional)
- 250ml rice milk/water

Calories	Protein	Carbohydrates	Fat
409	25.6g	31.7g	20g

Side Dishes_

Make up and refrigerate after use.

Cauliflower mash

- 1 large head cauliflower
- 1 tsp whole grain mustard
- 1 tbsp chopped parsley
- 1 clove garlic (optional)
- 1 tbsp olive oil or free range butter

Steam the cauliflower for 10-15 minutes. Then transfer to food processor, adding additional ingredients until smooth and creamy. Season to taste.

Calories	Protein	Carbohydrates	Fat
379	16.9g	45.7g	14.3g

Red cabbage and carrot salad

- 1/2 red cabbage (sliced)
- 2 large carrots (peeled and grated)
- 1 medium white onion (chopped)
- 1/4 cup raisins
- Any allowable sauce

Calories	Protein	Carbohydrates	Fat
337	8.5g	73.5g	1g

Mediterranean salad

- 1/2 bag mixed green leaves
- Medium sized red onion (chopped)
- 1 cucumber
- 1 large red tomato
- Tbsp red wine vinegar

Calories	Protein	Carbohydrates	Fat
120	4.8g	22.1g	1.4g

Fancy something naughty not on the plan but still healthy? Why not try one of these...

MK Healthy Option club pitta sandwich

- 1 x pitta bread
- 1 x 200g chicken breast (cooked and sliced)
- 2 x hard boiled eggs (sliced)
- 2 x spring onions (chopped)
- 1/4 iceberg lettuce
- 1 x tbsp light mayonnaise

Toast pitta bread under warm grill to make it easier to open up, layer all ingredients inside, cut in half and serve with side salad if necessary.

SERVES 1 – COOKING TIME 15 MINUTES

PER SERVING

Calories	Protein	Carbohydrates	Fat
284	28.5g	20g	10g

Warm chicken tikka wrap with mango chutney and cucumber and mint yoghurt

- 1 x 200g chicken breast (cooked)
- 2 x tortilla wraps
- 1 tsp mango chutney
- 1 tbsp greek yoghurt
- 1 x bunch mint (chopped)
- 1 x tsp tikka paste
- 1 x tbsp olive oil
- $^1/_6$ cucumber
- $^1/_2$ bag rocket

Chop cooked chicken into cubes and mix with olive oil and tikka paste, mix chopped mint with the yoghurt. Spread mango chutney over bottom half of tortilla wraps. Place chicken mix and rocket on top and roll, serve the yoghurt on the side.

SERVES 2 – COOKING TIME 15 MINUTES

PER SERVING

Calories	Protein	Carbohydrates	Fat
334	21.5g	23.9g	16.9g

Beef, horseradish and beetroot wrap with rocket

- 2 x tortilla wraps
- 1 x 100g beef fillet (stripped)
- 50g horseradish sauce
- 1 x bag rocket
- 100g packet cooked beetroot (diced)
- 1 x tbsp olive oil
- 2 x tbsp lemon juice
- Salt and pepper

Grill beef strips under a hot grill for 5 minutes or until cooked, with a little olive oil. Once cooked mix with diced beetroot, rocket, olive oil and lemon juice and roll in tortilla wrap, seal end of the wrap with the horseradish to make it stick.

SERVES 2 – COOKING TIME 15 MINUTES

PER SERVING

Calories	Protein	Carbohydrates	Fat
282	16.5g	18.5g	15.8g

Dressings_

Tracy Holly Everyday

The Everyday Healthy Salad Dressing is a vital component to good nutrition. It is extremely therapeutic and beneficial for optimum health and performance. The Everyday Healthy Salad Dressing acts as a digestive enzyme in the body, helps to ward off disease in the body, lubricates the joints and definitely satisfies the soul.

Make and store your dressing in a screw-top jar. Always remember to shake the jar vigorously to combine the dressing before using. The Everyday Healthy Salad Dressing can be refrigerated up to one week. Take out of the refrigerator before use to liquefy dressing and bring out the flavor.

Use this super savoury dressing to dress salads, marinate meat, fish or chicken, as a side sauce for meats or steamed vegetables, or as a dip for raw vegetables.

Together, in a glass screw top jar add:

- 1 part (1/2 cup-125 ml) 'extra virgin' olive oil
- 1 part (1/2 cup-125 ml) juice from freshly squeezed lemon
- 1 tbsp (15ml) dijon mustard
- 6 cloves of freshly grated garlic or 1 large clove elephant garlic

Makes approximately 1 cup (250ml) of dressing, shake vigorously. Taste. If you like it tarter, add more lemon juice, if you like it oilier add more oil. It's that easy!

For a change, I vary the Everyday Dressing by using flax seed oil instead of olive oil, balsamic vinegar or apple cider vinegar instead of lemon juice.

To make honey mustard dressing start with the Everyday Dressing and add 1 extra tbsp (15ml) of dijon and 2 tbsp (30ml) of unpasteurized honey.

OTHER CHOICES

Udo's flax oil, extra virgin olive oil, cider vinegar or red wine vinegar.

With thanks to Tracy Holly

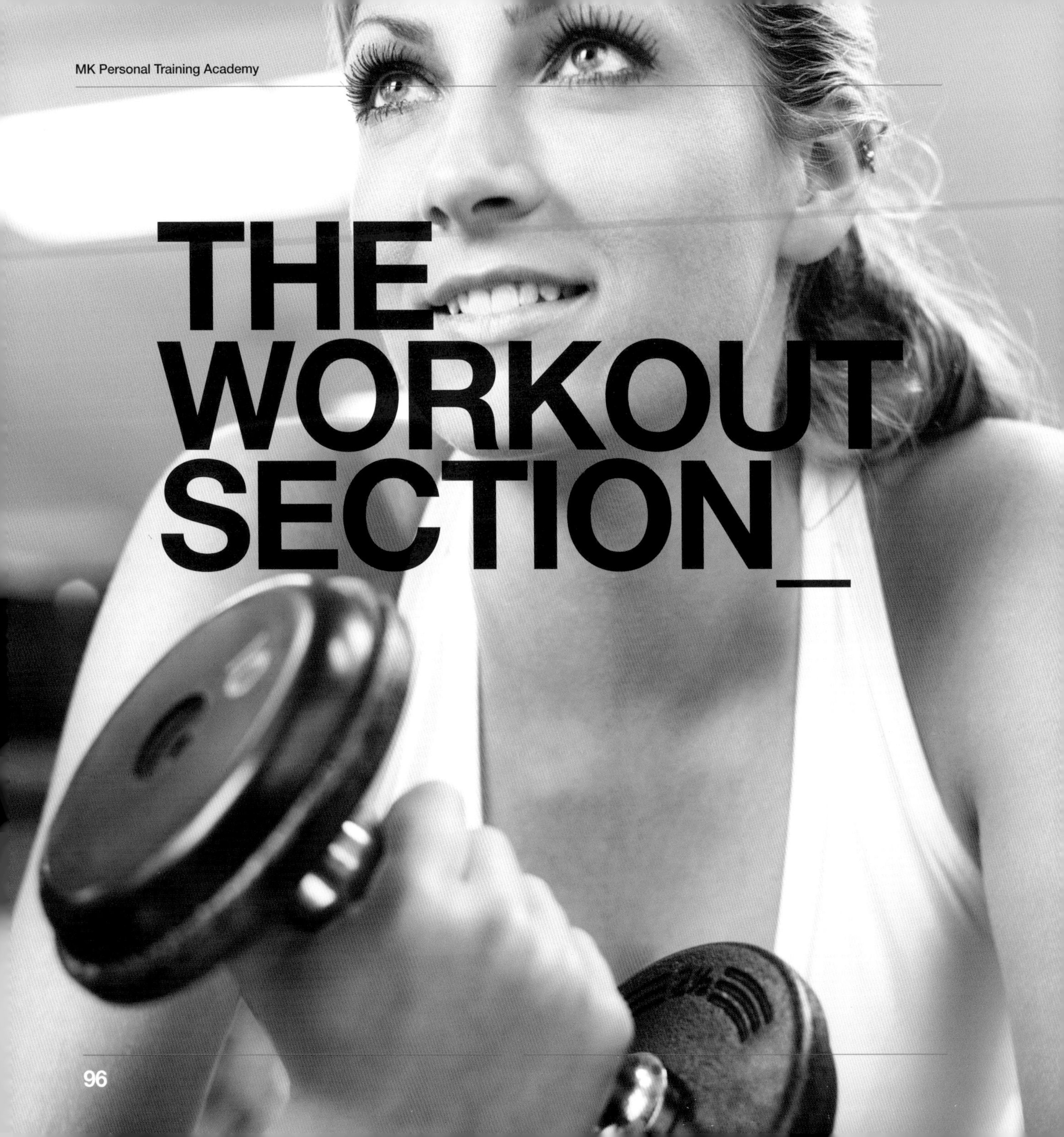

THE WORKOUT SECTION_

The workouts prepared for you in this book are based on the science of training for fat loss. We have chosen exercises that, through our experience with hundreds of clients at MK Personal Training Academy, target the most common posture problems, alleviate aching joints and burn bucket loads of calories.

Follow with passion.

Rate of Performed Exertion (RPE)

Level 1	Very Easy
Level 3	Easy
Level 5	Moderate
Level 7	Hard
Level 8	Extremely Hard
Level 9	Flat Out
Level 10	Game Over!

Taken from Borg Scale 6-20

your workout routine_

Always follow the simple steps below to maximise your workouts to be safe and effective:

1. *Mobility Set*
2. *Phase 1/2/3 Set*
3. *Interval Training Set*
4. *Flexibility Set*

interval training_

For many years aerobic training has been taken as the best way to burn lots of calories and lose fat. **Unfortunately this is simply not true.** Remember, the only tissue that burns fat in the body is muscle and aerobic work is possibly the least effective way to increase it. Our bodies adapt to everything we do, so as we burn lots of calories with aerobic training our clever body adapts by slowing down the metabolism to conserve energy. This is highlighted by the fact that people seem to do more and more for the same results. ***Sound familiar?***

Interval training is intense exercise with short rest periods, enabling you to do a much higher intensity of workout.

The work intervals can be made progressively harder and the rest intervals progressively shorter, as you progress and these workouts can always be done in short time periods. Helping us to spend less time in the gym for much quicker, better results, isn't that the point?

mobility_

The purpose of these mobility exercises is to warm up the body specifically for the workout ahead. These exercises are very good for the joints and can be done daily if you wish.

Opposite Arm / Leg Raise

Start with the hands underneath the shoulders (shoulder width apart) and knees under the hips (hip width apart) keeping your hips square and facing down reach out your opposite arm and leg keeping your tummy pulled in, hold for 5 seconds and repeat on the other side.
Repeat 10 times.

Bent Knee Twists

Start with feet together, lying on your back, arms out at your sides, palms up. Keeping your shoulder blades in contact with the floor at all times drop your knees from side to side. Repeat 10 times on each side.

Pilates Bridge

Start with feet hip width apart, keeping your tummy pulled in slowly start to peel off the floor from the tail bone first slowly up just past the shoulder blades and then peel back down again through the spine, hips and tailbone down last. Shoulders should be relaxed and feet straight, knees pointing to ceiling. Repeat 8-10 times.

Calf Band Mobility

Start lying on your back; have one knee bent with one foot on the floor. Take band around other foot reaching your leg up towards the ceiling keeping the band wide around foot, point your toes and then flex your foot towards you. Don't lock out the knee. Repeat on the other leg 10 times on each side.

Cat Camel

Start on all fours hands under shoulders and knees under hips (shoulder and hip width apart), round back up towards the ceiling keeping your tummy pulled in and then sticking the tailbone out, arch the back down bringing the head up allowing the spine to extend fully. Repeat 10 times.

phase 1_

These exercises should be performed in a circuit, one straight after the other, following the numbered order.

To be performed in weeks 1-4, 3 times a week.

***Care** – be careful not to push the lower back down.*

A1_ Lower Abs

Start lying on your back, knees bent, feet hip width apart. Begin with big deep breath in through nose fill up tummy. Slowly draw the belly button in towards the spine and up towards the chest. Exhale keeping the belly button in for 10 seconds. Repeat 10 times.

A2_ Ball Crunch

Start lying back over the ball, keeping your hips and back in contact with the ball, legs bent, feet hip width apart. Place tongue on roof of your mouth and slowly crunch up 30 degrees, pause and lower back 45 degrees over the ball. Repeat 20 times, lower down for 3 seconds, up for 1 second.

***Care** – keep the head and neck in line with the body as you crunch.*

A3_ Ball Squat

Start by placing the swiss ball against the wall, place into the small of your the back. Keep upright, feet hip width apart and slowly lower down pushing hips under the ball with your chest up and back straight. Once at 90 degrees, pause for a second and return to the start. Repeat 20 times, lower down for 3 seconds, up for 1 second.

A4_ Chest Supported Row

Start by lying face down on a swiss ball or incline bench. Hold dumbbells, palms down. Pull upwards at right angles squeezing your shoulder blades. Slowly lower back down to straight arms. Repeat 15 times, lift up for 1 second, lower down for 3 seconds.

A5_ Single Leg Deadlift

Start by standing on one leg, dumbbells at your sides. Keeping standing, leg slightly bent, slowly bend over, maintaining arch in the lower back push your hips back and keep the weight over your heel, as you return to the upright position squeeze your bottom. Repeat 20 times, lower down for 3 seconds, lift up for 1 second.

***Care** – don't allow the lower back to round.*

A6_ Push Up Plus

Start in the push up position, fully out on toes or modified on hands and knees, squeeze the shoulder blades together, release and drop into a push up, keeping your head aligned with the body. Return to the top and squeeze shoulder blades again. Repeat 15 times, lower down for 3 seconds, up for 1 second.

Easier Option

***Care** – don't lift up too high causing hyper-extension of the back.*

A7_ Ball Bridge

Start by lying on your back with your feet together up on the ball, arms out, palms up. Lift hips up to parallel keeping tummy drawn in, then slowly lower back down. Repeat 20 times, lift up for 1 second, down for 3 seconds.

A8_ Dumbbell Scaption

Start by standing feet hip width apart, dumbbells at your side. Slowly raise up to a 45 degree angle, thumbs pointing up first, to slightly above shoulder level. Slowly lower down at the same angle to the start position. Repeat 15 times, lift up for 1 second, lower down for 3 seconds.

After completing a full set of exercises rest for 60 seconds and repeat twice more.

Try not to rest between exercises longer than 30 seconds.

phase 1_ interval training

Choose any type of cardio machine – Bike, Treadmill, X-Trainer, Park!

Warm up for 3 minutes.

Perform 1 minute as fast as you can at the highest level you can (8-9 RPE) *See Chart.

Now perform 2 minutes at a steady, moderate pace to recover (4-5 RPE) *See Chart.

Repeat 2 more times.

Cool down for 3 minutes.

Total Time 15 minutes.

Perform this cardio interval training 3 times per week after your resistance training.

phase 2_

Focused exercises for weeks 5-8. To be performed 3-4 times a week.

A1_ Partial Lunge

Start with your feet hip width apart in a split stance with bent knees making sure the front knee isn't going too far over the front foot. Both feet should be straight; bend knees as low as possible and come back up to start position, keeping your knees bent. Repeat on the other side. Repeat 15 times, lower down for 3 seconds, lift up for 1 second.

A2_ Band Pull Downs

Start by holding a band above your head - pull the band outwards, your hands shoulder width apart. Arms straight, just behind head. Keeping the same resistance, bend your elbows until your arms come just below the ears - keeping the resistance and reaching your arms back up into the start position. Repeat 12 times, pull down for 1 second, release up for 3 seconds.

B1_ Ball Hamstring Curls

Starting with your feet on the ball, arms at your sides, keeping your feet together, lift your bottom straight off the floor. Keeping your bottom lifted, bring the ball towards you, bending the knees as your heels come towards your bottom and then take your legs straight out again, keeping your bottom lifted back to the start position. Repeat 15 times, ball in for 1 second, ball out for 3 seconds.

B2_ Ball Dumbbell Chest Press

Start by lying with your head and shoulders on the ball, making sure that your knees are over your feet in a table top position. Holding the weights at chest height, press your arms up keeping your arms over your chest, straightening your arms slowly and then return your arms back down to the start position. Repeat 12 times, lower down for 3 seconds, push up for 1 second.

C1_ Reverse Lunge – Dumbbell Opposite Shoulder

Start with your feet hip width apart holding a dumbbell at your right shoulder. Step back into a split stance with right leg forward, bend both knees making sure that the front knee doesn't go too far over your front foot. Repeat on the other side and change the dumbbell to the other hand. Repeat 15 times, lower down for 3 seconds, back up for 1 second.

C2_ Dumbbell Reverse Flys

Start lying face down on a ball or bench, arms down at shoulder level, palms facing. Slowly lift the dumbbells outwards and upwards to shoulder height, pause and return to the start. Repeat 12 times, lift up for 1 second, lower down for 3 seconds.

D1_ Side ISO Abs

Start by lying on your side with your elbow under your shoulder. Take your legs into a straight line keeping your hips even. Lift your hips off the floor and lower. (An easier option is to have your knees more bent.) Repeat 15 times, lift up 1 second, lower down for 3 seconds.

Easier Option

D2_ Forward Ball Rows

Start on your knees hands together on ball, keeping the back straight, slowly ease your body forward as one unit to a point where you are able to maintain perfect posture without the rest of your body contacting the ball. Keep the same position as you return to the start. Repeat 15 times, forward for 3 seconds, back for 1 second.

The first two exercises should be done one after the other and then repeat 2 times.

Try to keep the rest period to 30 seconds between each.

Follow this format for all 8 exercises in pairs.

phase 2_ interval training

Choose any type of cardio machine – Bike, Treadmill, X-Trainer, Park!

Warm up for 3 minutes.

Perform 1 minute as fast as you can at the highest level you can (8-9 RPE) *See Chart.

Now perform 2 minutes at a steady, moderate pace to recover (4-5 RPE) *See Chart.

Repeat 3 more times.

Cool down for 3 minutes.

Total Time 18 minutes.

Perform this cardio interval training 3-4 times per week after your resistance training.

phase 3_

Intensive exercises for weeks 9-12. To be performed 4 times a week.

***Care** – only squat to a position where you don't bend forward or allow your knees to cross over your toes.*

A1_ Squat

Start by standing feet hip width apart. Bring dumbbells up to your shoulders with palms facing towards you. Slowly squat down, pushing your hips out, keeping your weight over your heels. Chest up, back straight. Once at 90 degrees or close to, return to start position bringing hips through at the top. Repeat 10 times, lower down for 2 seconds, up for 1 second.

A2_ Dumbbell Bent Over Row

Start with your feet hip width apart, push your hips back and bend over, maintaining an arch in your lower back. Hold this position and pull dumbbells upwards towards you 90 degrees, squeezing your shoulders. Slowly lower the dumbbells back down. Repeat 10 times, pull up for 1 seconds, back down for 2 second.

A3_ Deadlift

Start by standing feet hip width apart, dumbbells at the side of your body. Push your hips back and bend as low as possible while maintaining a strict curve in your lower back. As you return up to the start position, squeeze your bottom through the movement. Repeat 10 times, lower down for 2 seconds, back up for 1 second.

***Care** – be careful not to round your back off as you bend.*

A4_ Ball Push Up

Easier Option

***Care** – don't allow your lower back to drop into too much arch or round off the upper back.*

Start (dependent on option) by placing your thighs or feet onto the ball keeping your body in alignment. Slowly lower into a push up position keeping your chest between your hands and your head in line. Pause and return to the start position. Repeat 10 times, lower down for 2 seconds, back up for 1 second.

Care *– don't allow the front knee to stray inwards, try and keep over the second toe.*

B1_ Bulgarian Split Squat

Start by placing your back foot up onto a step and front foot forward, hip width apart. Slowly lower down as far as possible – back knee ideally just off the floor. Keeping the weight on the front heel push back up to the start position. Repeat 20 times, lower down for 2 seconds, back up for 1 second.

B2_ Dumbbell Military Press

Start by standing feet hip width apart, dumbbells at shoulder height, slightly forward. Slowly press dumbbells above your head bringing in at the top. Lower back down to the start. Repeat 20 times, press up for one second, lower down for 2 seconds.

Tip – as you press up, keep your legs slightly bent, tummy drawn in not allowing the hips to push forward.

C1_ Woodchops

Start by standing with your feet wide apart. Grab the cable or tubing handle with opposite hand first. Keeping your arms straight 'chop' in a diagonal pattern high to low, twisting from the waist, not the hips. Slowly return to the start position. Repeat 20 times, chop down for 1 second, chop back for 2 seconds.

Tip – pivoting one leg to the other helps place more emphasis on the waist.

Note – if training at home use tubing and door attachment.

C2_ Ball Jackknife

Start as in the ball push up position, with nice straight body alignment. Draw the ball inwards until under your hips, keeping the arch in your lower back and tummy drawn in. Return to the start position. Repeat 20 times, pull in for 1 second, push out for 2 seconds.

The first 4 exercises should be done one after another, 3 times with 45 seconds rest between each set.

The next 2 exercises should be done one after another 3 times with 45 seconds rest between each set.

The last 2 exercises should be done one after another 3 times with 45 seconds rest between each set.

phase 3_ interval training

Choose any type of cardio machine – Bike, Treadmill, X-Trainer, Park!

Warm up for 3 minutes.

Perform 1 minute as fast as you can at the highest level you can (8-9 RPE) **See Chart.*

Now perform 2 minutes at a steady, moderate pace to recover (4-5 RPE) **See Chart.*

Repeat 4 more times.

Cool down for 3 minutes.

Total Time 21 minutes.

Perform this cardio interval training 4 times per week after your resistance training.

flexibility_

A very important but often overlooked aspect of fitness is flexibility. At MK Lifefit we believe the best time to stretch muscles is at the end of the workout, when they are nice and warm. We have chosen the muscle groups we know need particular attention after training.

Start/Finish

Midpoint

Neck Extensors

Start by standing back straight, tummy pulled in. Turn your head 45% to the right, drop your chin to the chest and take your right hand over the top of the head and apply a little pressure until you feel a stretch down the back of the neck, hold for about 30-45 seconds and repeat on the other side.

Pecs

Start by taking your right arm 90 degrees against a wall, step forward with your right leg, looking ahead, ease your body forward stretching the chest and shoulder. Hold for 30-45 seconds.

Glutes

Start by lying on your back, knees bent hip width apart. Take your right foot across your left knee, holding around your left leg, bring your leg off the floor towards you, feeling a stretch on your right side, hold for 30-45 seconds, repeat on other side. If you find it hard to reach then use a band around your leg and knee.

Start/Finish

Midpoint

Hamstrings

Start by lying on your back, take a band around your right foot keeping your left knee bent, keeping your elbows in and in contact with the floor, straighten your leg feeling a stretch behind your knee as you try to bring your leg a bit closer towards your body, hold for 30-45 seconds. Repeat on other side.

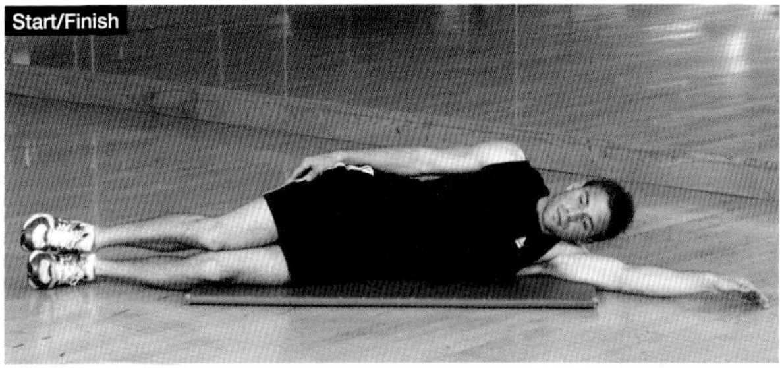
Start/Finish

Midpoint

Quads

Start by lying on your side, keeping your legs together take your hand around your foot and hold the stretch for 30-45 seconds, bringing your other knee forward and pushing your hips forward slightly. Repeat on other side.

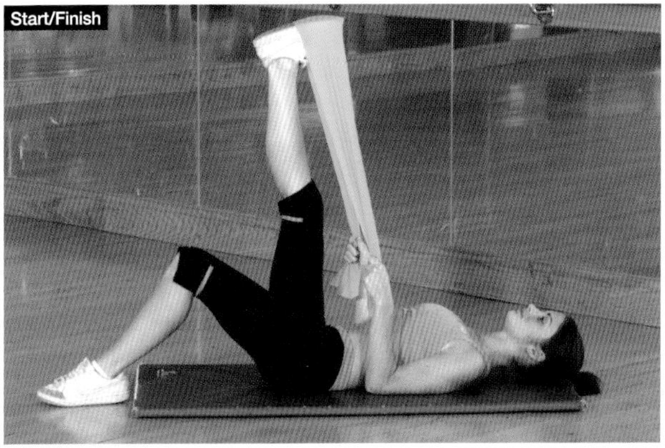
Start/Finish

the mklifefit. express workout_

Imagine the length of a 60 minute aerobic session in 4 minutes.

The catch – it's very tough!

Based on the works of Dr Izumi Tabata an exercise scientist in Japan, who alongside his research team experimented with exercise intervals to discover how to increase both anaerobic and aerobic capacity at the same time.

It is very effective for fat loss and only takes 4 minutes!

Take one exercise, eg. Bike, Run, Step Up, Squat, etc. and perform the following:

20 seconds as many repetitions as possible.

10 seconds rest.

Repeat 7 more times.

If on The Bike the 20 seconds should be a very high level of resistance as fast as humanly possible! Followed by 10 seconds at an easy resistance and a steady pace.

enjoy!

SYNCRO
SPORTESSE

Why Personal Training?

maybe a better question to ask is why not?

If you are unable to visit us, don't worry, we can offer individual coaching online or by telephone.

At **MK Personal Training Academy** we believe the main reasons that hold people back from experiencing the true benefits of one to one exercise are:

- cost
- people feel intimidated
- people don't realise the true difference between a personal training program and a gym program
- people believe they know what to do
- the pressure from a personal trainer

By listing these reasons, we want to show you that we understand your concerns. We are very passionate about reaching out to as many of you as possible to show that the reasons for not embarking on a personal training program are unfounded.

We offer cost effective packages with plenty of flexibility to suit.

An initial assessment to help you learn about what you need coupled with your own personal goals is where the journey begins...

Call us today on 0870 442 7115 quoting 'lifefit001' to receive a FREE health assessment from one of our personal training professionals.

resources_

1. **MK Personal Training Academy:**
   www.mkpersonaltraining.co.uk
   Tel/Fax: 0870 442 7115

2. MK Lifefit Natural Health Products:
   www.mkpersonaltraining.co.uk
   Tel/Fax: 0870 442 7115

3. **Home Exercise Kit:** call **MK Personal Training Academy** 0870 442 7115 and quote MK Lifefit Home

4. The Punchbowl: Lapworth, Solihull
   Great Gastro Pub/Restaurant with **MK Personal Training Academy** healthy option
   www.punchbowllapworth.co.uk

5. The Hurdles: Brockbridge, Droxford
   Creator of the recipe section Gareth Cole's restaurant
   www.thehurdles.co.uk

6. www.coryholly.com
   Premiere Sports Nutrition, Health and Fitness Education

7. Reverse Osmosis: Grandie Marketing, 225 Main Road, Northampton NN5 8PR. Tel: 01604 752838

8. Liquid Egg Whites
   www.eggnation.co.uk

9. The Doctors Lab
   Full comprehensive blood tests available by medical laboratory
   www.tdlpathology.com

10. www.mercola.com – fantastic website full of healthy information

your notes_